Leading

Effective Meetings, Teams, and Work Groups

in Districts and Schools

Matthew Jennings

Association for Supervision and Curriculum Development
Alexandria, Virginia USA

Association for Supervision and Curriculum Development
1703 N. Beauregard St. • Alexandria, VA 22311-1714 USA
Phone: 800-933-2723 or 703-578-9600 • Fax: 703-575-5400
Web site: www.ascd.org • E-mail: member@ascd.org
Author guidelines: www.ascd.org/write

Gene R. Carter, *Executive Director;* Nancy Modrak, *Director of Publishing;* Julie Houtz, *Director of Book Editing & Production;* Ernesto Yermoli, *Project Manager;* Cathy Guyer, *Senior Graphic Designer;* Valerie Younkin, *Desktop Publishing Specialist;* Vivian Coss, *Production Specialist*

PAPERBACK ISBN: 978-1-4166-0538-6   ASCD product #107088   s6/07

Also available as an e-book through ebrary, netLibrary, and many online booksellers (see Books in Print for the ISBNs).

Quantity discounts for the paperback edition only: 10–49 copies, 10%; 50+ copies, 15%; for 1,000 or more copies, call 800-933-2723, ext. 5634, or 703-575-5634. For desk copies: member@ascd.org.

Library of Congress Cataloging-in-Publication Data
Jennings, Matthew.
    Leading effective meetings, teams, and work groups in districts and schools / Matthew Jennings.
        p. cm.
    Includes bibliographical references and index.
    ISBN 978-1-4166-0538-6 (pbk. : alk. paper)   1. Meetings—United States—Planning.   2. Teaching teams—United States.   3. Teachers—Professional relationships—United States.   4. School management and organization—United States.   I. Title.

    LB1751.J46 2007
    371.2'07--dc22

                                                                                            2007005529

18 17 16 15 14 13 12 11 10 09 08 07   1 2 3 4 5 6 7 8 9 10 11 12

Leading Effective Meetings, Teams, and Work Groups in Districts and Schools

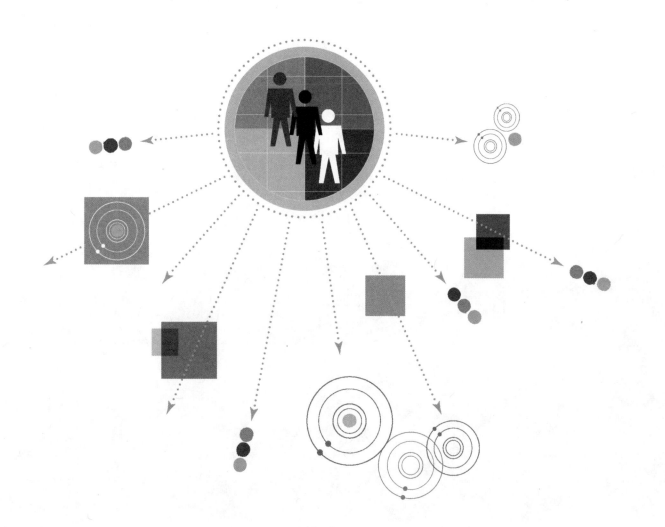

Section 1

Faculty Meetings

Introduction

In my experience as both a graduate education professor and a school district administrator, I have asked many teachers what they thought of school faculty meetings—and not once did I ever receive a favorable reply. Most of the time, my questions provoked emotions ranging from indifference to contempt; teachers perceive faculty meetings as wastes of time to be tolerated, and nothing more.

The good news is that educational leaders can make faculty meetings better; they don't have to continue facilitating meetings that accomplish little or nothing. Because running effective meetings is not taught in most school administrator preparation programs, I set out to write this book with the goals of synthesizing the available research and translating it into action steps that you can take. Using the information and activities contained in this section will change your meetings from dreaded events to major sources of learning, social support, and dialogue.

1 | Planning and Preparing for Faculty Meetings

Knowing is not enough; we must apply. Willing is not enough; we must do.

—Goethe

Mr. Smith was recently appointed as superintendent of his school district. In an effort to orient himself to the district, he made it a point to have informal conversations with faculty and with members of the community. Through these conversations, Mr. Smith found that Mrs. Greene, one of the district's eight elementary school principals, was consistently described as an outstanding leader. Curious, he decided to pay her a visit.

As fate would have it, Mr. Smith arrived at Mrs. Greene's school just as she was about to start her faculty meeting. He decided to wait for her to finish so that they could have their conversation afterwards. When he took a seat, he was immediately surprised at the room arrangement: instead of the traditional rows of chairs facing front, there were tables with four chairs at each. He thought to himself that this was an invitation to trouble—teachers would be just like the kids and talk to each other the whole time Mrs. Greene was talking. He also noticed there were refreshments on a table near the side of the room. He wondered if they were celebrating something special. In the front of the room was a poster titled "Faculty Meeting Ground Rules." These rules seemed like an interesting idea. He wanted to see if the staff members would follow them throughout the course of the meeting.

A few minutes after students were dismissed, staff members began to arrive at the meeting. Mr. Smith was struck by how many teachers arrived before the meeting started with smiles on their faces. After allowing a few minutes for staff to get refreshments and engage in informal conversation, Mrs. Greene started the meeting by quickly reviewing the agenda. Next, she asked staff members to engage in what she called a "staff building" activity; then to engage in "team building" activities at each table; and finally to engage in a combination of small- and large-group activities related to the use of technology in achieving math and reading goals.

Mr. Smith was struck by the nature of the conversations at the meeting: everyone appeared to be actively listening and passionately sharing ideas while remaining focused on the topic under discussion. Mr. Smith had never seen anything like this; it struck him that the meeting resembled some of the better classroom lessons he'd observed as a principal.

When the meeting was over, Mr. Smith met with Mrs. Greene. After revealing how dreadful many of the meetings he'd both led and attended had been, he wanted to know how she had managed to create such a productive and stimulating experience. Her answer was so simple that it surprised him. She said that she ran her faculty meetings like she had run her classrooms: she laid the foundation for success in the beginning of the year, then planned each meeting as carefully as she did her lessons as a teacher.

The Foundation for Effective School Faculty Meetings

Either prior to or at the beginning of the school year, you must

- Communicate the purpose of faculty meetings.
- Collaborate with staff on developing norms for expected behavior.
- Create faculty "base teams."

Communicating the Purpose of Faculty Meetings

Meetings shouldn't simply serve as forums for transmitting information to staff; this should be done via memo, weekly bulletin, or e-mail prior to each meeting. Instead, meetings should fulfill the following three purposes:

1. **To build relationships among staff.** Many teachers feel isolated from their colleagues, which can in turn make them feel alienated from their work. Building relationships with colleagues is necessary for them to feel engaged.

2. **To focus on professional development.** Because faculty meetings are among the few occasions when the entire staff is together, they provide a precious opportunity for systematically building the instructional capacity of teachers.

3. **To solve problems and make decisions.** Sometimes, critical decisions require input from the entire school community. When structured appropriately, faculty meetings can provide a forum for this input.

You should communicate the above three meeting goals to staff members in a memo before the school year starts. Here's an example:

To: All school staff
From: Mr. Jennings
Date: 9/01/07
Subject: School faculty meetings

Although they may not have always seemed so in the past, faculty meetings are valuable opportunities for our professional learning community. These meetings are among the few times our entire staff is together. In order to make our meeting time valuable, I have decided to institute the following changes:

1. All information that can be shared in writing prior to the meeting will be included in the weekly staff bulletin. Staff members are responsible for reading this bulletin and seeking clarification when necessary.
2. Instead of information transmission, our faculty meetings will now emphasize relationship building, professional development, and problem solving and decision making.
3. If we do not have an activity that meets the criteria in #2 above, we will not have a faculty meeting.

I realize this new format may make some of you uncomfortable. To let go of the way we always do things and try something new requires us to take a risk. The long-term benefits of this change will be worth it for us as a staff and our students. If you have any questions, please stop by and see me.

Collaborating with Staff on Developing Norms for Expected Behavior

Clearly articulated and agreed-upon norms contribute to an atmosphere of trust, which is itself essential for successful collaboration. At the first faculty meeting of the year, you should facilitate the collaborative development of such norms, which will be based on the values, expectations, and past experiences of staff members. The following activity can help you to accomplish this task.

Step 1. Begin by facilitating a discussion of group norms. Example: "We have all been part of a team. In any team there are certain rules or expectations for how we will behave. What were some of the rules or expectations on teams on which you've served? What are some of the behaviors, both positive and negative, that you have experienced on a team?" Record the responses on a T-chart.

Step 2. Discuss the messages that the behaviors listed on the T-chart send to other team members.

Step 3. Discuss the value of having a set of basic agreements for faculty meetings. After reviewing a sample of possible agreements, have staff members add more to the list. Continue adding possible agreements until nobody can think of any more. Sample agreements could include the following:

• We will start and end meetings on time.
• We will actively listen to each other's ideas and opinions.
• We will make important decisions through consensus.

• We will work from a staff-developed agenda that is distributed 24 hours prior to the staff meeting.

• We will remain focused on the topic or task.

Step 4. Have staff members divide a piece of paper into two columns. Inform staff members that they each have 100 points, which they must divide among all the agreements listed. (The more points, the more valuable the agreement.) Once staff members have all completed the task individually, ask them to share their scores in groups of three or four and complete the activity once more. When everyone is finished, collect and tally the second set of scores. The top three to five choices will then constitute the group's agreements for faculty meetings.

It is often necessary to remind staff members of the established agreements, either verbally at the beginning of a staff meeting or in the form of a poster prominently displayed in the meeting room.

Creating Faculty "Base Teams"

Base teams are long-term, heterogeneous groups to which staff members are assigned. The major purposes of these base groups are as follows:

• To involve all staff members at the beginning and ending of each meeting
• To personalize meetings
• To provide a schoolwide focus to meetings
• To provide peer support for and celebration of staff efforts
• To increase the likelihood that all staff members will actively contribute to the meeting

Base teams should have between two and five staff members, with four being optimal because it allows for pair work. You can assign members at random, or choose to include a mix of grades, subject areas, or experience levels on each team. Either way, teams should be relatively heterogeneous and represent more than one grade level or subject area. (To keep things fresh, be sure to disband the teams and form new ones after every six to ten meetings.) At a minimum, teams will meet at the beginning of each meeting to celebrate a teaching success from the previous week, and at the end of each meeting to summarize the proceedings.

Faculty Meeting Roles

Any group will function more effectively if members know each other's responsibilities. The following are the three most common roles at faculty meetings:

• **The facilitator** is usually (but not always) the principal. He or she leads the meeting and promotes the participation of all members through gate keeping and consensus seeking. (Essential facilitation skills are addressed in Chapter 2.)
• **The recorder** writes down details of the meeting, such as the people present and the agenda items, along with any relevant information discussed. He or she should also produce written minutes of the meeting and distribute them to all staff members within 48 hours.
• **The timekeeper** watches the clock and warns fellow members when the designated time for each agenda item is over.

Whether these roles are permanent or rotate is up to you. Permanent assignments have the advantage of consistency and of helping staff members develop role-specific skills over time. Rotating assignments have the advantage of promoting equal responsibility among all staff members for all roles.

Developing the Meeting Agenda

A meeting agenda provides staff members with a guide to the proceedings and encourages them to focus on upcoming tasks. Without an agenda, staff members may have trouble discerning the meeting's purpose.

When teachers help shape the agenda, they gain an increased sense of ownership for the meeting. Be sure to set a deadline by which teachers must provide topics in advance. When submitting items, teachers should include their names, the topics they wish to address, and the resources and approximate amount of time that they will require.

A quality meeting agenda should include the following:

- The overall purpose of the meeting in one or two clearly written sentences
- A note on who is required to attend
- The projected time span of the meeting
- The location of the meeting
- Any special resources that participants should bring
- Any advance preparation that is required
- The names of the recorder and timekeeper for the meeting

- Agenda items, preferably including questions to encourage advance reflection (e.g., "How can we cut our proposed budget by 10 percent without harming our instructional program?"), along with the projected time span for discussing each item

Figure 1.1 shows a sample meeting agenda. Although not strictly necessary, it is often helpful to share a rough draft of the agenda with staff representatives prior to distributing it, for proofreading and feedback. Whenever possible, staff members

---

1.1 Sample Meeting Agenda

Columbia School Faculty Meeting

Purpose: To celebrate our current successes implementing cooperative learning and to identify areas requiring additional assistance or training

Required Attendees: All teachers

Optional Attendees: Student teachers and paraprofessional staff

Date: October 8   **Time**: 3:45 – 4:30   **Location**: Team Room 2A

Required Materials: Cooperative learning journal, pen or pencil

Advance Preparation: Please read the small-group discussion questions below and reflect on your answers.

Recorder: Jane S.   **Timekeeper**: Ralph R.

Agenda Items:
Base teams meeting (5 minutes)
- Staff-building activity

Small-group discussion of the following questions: (20 minutes)
- What cooperative learning strategies have worked successfully for you?
- What problems are you having with implementing cooperative learning strategies in our classrooms?
- What cooperative learning strategies would you like to learn more about?

Large-group sharing of small-group responses (15 minutes)

Base teams meeting (5 minutes)
- Review of next steps and responsibilities
- Team celebration

should receive the agenda at least 24 hours before the meeting.

Physical Setting

Participants will contribute more to and get more out of meetings if the physical setting is comfortable and conducive to achieving the meeting's objectives. Here are a few guidelines to consider in this respect.

➤ **Seating arrangements**. These must be matched to the types of activities that will occur at the meeting:

• A U-shape or semicircle arrangement is best for groups of 12 to 22 staff members, and is well suited to large-group discussion.
• A single square or round is best for groups of 8 to 12 staff members, and is well suited to problem solving.
• A V-shape arrangement with tables of four to five participants apiece facing the front of the room is best for groups of 16 to 40. This arrangement is well suited to small-group work at each table.
• A traditional arrangement of front-facing rows is appropriate for any size group, and is particularly well suited to the imparting of information by the facilitator.

➤ **Room temperature**. Though often overlooked, setting an appropriate room temperature is essential for a comfortable meeting environment. Most people find the optimal temperature to be between 68 and 72 degrees. If weather conditions permit, you can provide additional air circulation by opening doors and windows.

➤ **Lighting**. Bright but indirect natural lighting is best; whenever possible keep blinds open to take advantage of the sun. (Low light makes work hard on the eyes and the nervous system, and can induce drowsiness.)

➤ **Music**. People respond well to appropriate music. Not only does it connect with them emotionally, but it also helps to break their normal thought patterns. Music within the range of 65 to 80 beats per minute is best for setting a positive mood. Use familiar tunes and songs in major keys (e.g., "Don't Worry, Be Happy" by Bobby McFerrin).

➤ **Smell**. Aromas can powerfully influence the mood of a meeting: whereas peppermint, lemon, and cinnamon scents enhance alertness, for instance, lavender, orange, and rose scents encourage relaxation. If real estate agents are convinced that the smell of freshly baked bread can sway potential home buyers, then perhaps the smell of freshly baked cookies can positively influence meeting attendees.

➤ **Color**. Color affects everyone. Hang colorful visuals and peripherals in the room to subtly enhance the mood of the room, and encourage the use of colored markers or pencils for completing activities, as this is likely to energize participants. Different colors are associated with different emotions:

• Red evokes anger, intensity, and danger. Use this color to highlight warnings.

• Yellow evokes happiness, cheerfulness, and warmth. Use this color when generating ideas and supporting creativity.
• Blue evokes reliability, trust, and tranquility. Use this color early and regularly in meetings to establish and reinforce trust.
• Green evokes productivity, growth, and forward momentum. Use this color when striving for compromise or consensus.
• Orange evokes energy, enthusiasm, and positive thinking. Use this color to highlight a subject or demonstrate connections between ideas.
• White evokes honesty and innocence. Use this color when striving for clarity and order.
• Black evokes independence, seriousness, and finality. *Do not* use black when brainstorming.

➤ **Refreshments.** Refreshments can provide attendees with a physical and psychological boost. This is particularly important because most faculty meetings occur after school, when energy levels are low. Food and drink can also facilitate community building by encouraging socialization among participants. For meetings lasting 30 minutes or less, snacks that are high in sugar (fruit, candy) are acceptable; however, because too much sugar can lead to drowsiness after a while, meetings lasting longer than 30 minutes should include foods that are high in protein (lean meat, yogurt) or complex carbohydrates (nuts, whole grain bread).

2

Facilitating Faculty Meetings

When teachers share information with each other and work together in the best interest of their students, good things happen.   —Susan Wheelan

As a leader, you must model the same types of behaviors when facilitating meetings that you expect teachers to develop in classrooms. Be sure to arrive at the meeting location early and prepared, for example, and to review the setup of the room beforehand. Just as teachers will often stand at the doors of their classrooms and greet each student as he or she enters, so too should you greet all meeting attendees. Make eye contact and welcome each teacher by name.

Skills and Guidelines

Before your first meeting gets under way, be sure to brush up on the following skills and guidelines to ensure the best possible conditions.

Oral Presentation Skills

When you present information at a meeting, participants will register not just your content, but also your presentation style. It is therefore critical that you pay attention to the quality of your delivery. Be sure to consider the following factors:

• **Volume and pitch**. Use a softer or louder voice to indicate urgency, exasperation, or importance.

• **Pace**. Like volume and pitch, variations in pace—for example, drawing certain words out more slowly than others—can signal that what is being said is especially noteworthy.

• **Pauses**. Judiciously placed pauses can focus the audience's attention and help members to process the speaker's message.

• **Pronunciation**. Enunciating clearly is critical if your audience is to understand your message. Among the most common mistakes in this regard are running words together and trailing off at the ends of sentences.

• **Fillers**. Words like "um," "ah," "okay," and "you know" can grate on listeners' nerves, so work diligently to eliminate them from your speech.

Discussion Skills

Use the following basic techniques to stimulate thinking during discussions:

• **Clarifying**. If you are unclear about what someone has said or think that staff members may be unclear, ask the speaker to explain what he or she means. (Example: "We would really like to understand your view on this issue. Can you explain it differently so that we can get a better understanding?")

• **Summarizing**. Every so often, summarize what has been said so far at the meeting for the group, making sure to ask if everyone agrees with your summary. (Example: "So far we have agreed on reducing the textbook budget by 5

percent and reallocating those funds for professional development. Does that sound accurate to all of you?")

• **Leading**. This technique is effective for introducing new topics or moving discussions forward. (Example: "Now that we have brainstormed possible solutions to this problem, are we ready to make a decision?")

• **Challenging**. Use this technique to question underlying assumptions or unstated biases that are keeping the group from moving forward. (Example: "Are we sure that we cannot hire substitute teachers to rotate among staff so that we can create common planning time?")

• **Stretching**. This is an effective technique for pushing a group to think differently about a situation. (Example: "Have we considered other possible ways to assess student progress in math? What about the possibility of portfolio assessment?")

• **Connecting**. Use this technique to share information or strategies that the group isn't using. (Example: "Janice, last year you had an interdisciplinary unit of study that combined art and math. Please share with the group the process you used to create this project.")

• **Integrating**. This technique can be used to merge ideas and conversations into an integrated whole. (Example: "The situation you are describing is similar to the one we discussed near the end of last week's meeting.")

Listening Skills

Active listening is hard work, because we usually listen only long enough to hear what we need to make our next point of agreement or disagreement.

This is especially true in staff meetings due to time pressure and fatigue from the day's work. Follow these recommendations to improve active listening in your meetings:

- Refrain from interrupting the person who is speaking.
- Don't be afraid of silence.
- If there is not enough time to listen actively, say so.
- Try not to be influenced by your feelings or biases about who is speaking.
- Paraphrase: listen to what is being said without distraction, then summarize what you heard and understood. (Example: "I think I hear you saying that there are limited fashions available to adolescents in stores today.")
- Check with speakers to make sure that your interpretation of what you've heard is correct. (Example: "It sounds like you don't think our proposed school dress code will work because of the limited fashions available to adolescents in stores. Is this correct?")
- Probe to expand on ideas, unearth assumptions, and explore applications. (Example: "May I ask what led you to that conclusion?")

Nonverbal Behaviors

The four principal types of nonverbal behavior in a faculty meeting are eye contact, facial expression, body position, and hand gestures:

- **Eye contact.** Whereas averting your eyes expresses disinterest and dislike, direct eye contact communicates interest and helps you establish a rapport with audience members. When presenting information at meetings, avoid looking at the ceiling or floor or over your audience's heads. Instead, make a conscious effort to scan the whole room and establish eye contact with everyone. When others are speaking, make direct eye contact with them. When responding to someone, begin by looking that person in the eye and then make eye contact with the rest of the audience.
- **Facial expression.** If you want to put staff members at ease, the first thing to do is smile, as this indicates warmth and openness in communication. Speakers who smile when appropriate are perceived as more intelligent and credible than those who do not, but only when the smiles are perceived as genuine (Friend & Cook, 2007). Obviously, smiling when trying to deliver a somber message can create confusion.
- **Body position.** Good posture conveys poise and confidence. When speaking to staff members, plant your feet on the ground and avoid shifting your weight back and forth. Walking among the audience can be a good idea, but pacing back and forth in the same spot is distracting.
- **Hand gestures.** Certain types of hand gestures—keeping your palms open when discussing goals, for example—convey openness, but be sure to avoid fidgeting with objects or keeping your hands in your pockets.

Visual Aids

A picture may be worth a thousand words, but which words is that picture communicating? To be effective, visual aids in staff meetings must be appropriate to the content being presented and must be of high quality. Communicating a message both visually and verbally increases the probability that staff members will remember it.

When designing visual aids, keep in mind the following guidelines:

• Page orientation (landscape or portrait) should be consistent.
• Words should be large enough for everyone to read.
• Variances in size and boldness of type should be consistent and make sense.
• Print should be in both upper- and lowercase type and in a sans-serif font.
• Use bullets to set off key points.
• Limit the number of different ideas on any one visual to a maximum of four.
• Make sure all staff members can see the visuals. Do not block staff members' view.
• Use a pointer to focus attention on main points.
• Orient staff members to the visual aid (e.g., "Here are three research-based guidelines for teaching new vocabulary words.")
• When speaking, address your audience rather than the visual aid.
• For slide show, overhead, and audiovisual presentations, turn off the lights immediately in front of the screen but keep them on in the rest of the room.

Computer Slide Show Guidelines

• Select a graphic or theme and stick with it throughout the design of the presentation.
• Employ a design template that uses as little of the entire screen as possible.
• Follow the eight-by-eight rule: use a maximum of eight words across and eight lines down each slide.
• When presenting lists, design the slide so that one line can be revealed at a time.
• To emphasize an item, make it a different color than the rest.
• Headings should be in 44-point type, and body text should be between 24- and 32-point type.
• Use one type of transition between all slides.
• Limit colors to two per slide (plus black).
• Ensure that there is enough contrast between typeface and background. Most audience members prefer a light typeface on a dark background.
• When transitioning to a new topic or pausing for an activity, have the slide fade to black.
• Don't overuse clip art, animations, or sound effects.

Overhead Transparency Guidelines

• Use graphics to highlight important ideas.
• Add a frame around the content of each transparency.
• Follow the eight-by-eight rule.
• Use clear, descriptive headings and subheadings.
• Use colors for emphasis, but avoid yellow as it doesn't show on transparencies.
• Number the transparencies for easy ordering.

Flip Chart Guidelines

• Consider boxing or underlining the heading on each chart.
• Make letters one to three inches tall.
• Have 10 lines or fewer per page.
• Use color consistently (e.g., dark colors for

words and bright colors to highlight).
• When recording participant statements, write on every other page so that staff members cannot read through to the next page.
• Use sticky notes to locate specific information on prepared charts.
• Test your markers to make sure they work before the staff meeting.
• Use water-based makers—they don't bleed through paper, and if you drop them on your clothes, the color washes out.
• Pencil small cues for yourself in the margins of the flip chart.
• Turn the page out of sight when the information is no longer pertinent.

Audiovisual Presentation Guidelines

• Cue up the DVD or video and check the sound level before the meeting.
• Show only whatever is required to make your point.
• Prior to starting the film, inform staff members of what they are expected to do during the viewing (e.g., take notes, watch for specific behaviors).
• Do not turn off all the lights if staff members are to take notes.
• Rewind the video following, not during, the meeting.

Base Team Activities

At the beginning of each meeting, base team members should complete a brief team-building activity, such as in the following examples:

• Each team member discusses a teaching success that he or she has had that week.
• Each team member completes an unfinished statement that you've provided (e.g., "If I weren't a teacher, I would be . . . " or "My favorite holiday is . . .").
• Each team creates a chant or cheer.
• Team members softly toss a small beanbag or Koosh-type ball to each other. Each time team members receive the ball, they name something for which they are grateful or compliment another team member.
• Team members reflect on a topic that you've provided—"a joyful experience," for example, or "a great adventure"—and jot down relevant questions to ask teammates. Each team member then takes a turn being interviewed on the topic by the rest of the team.
• Team members work together to solve a brainteaser.

Staff-Building Activities

To achieve a true professional learning community, you must devote attention to staff building. At a minimum, you should facilitate staff-building activities at meetings once a month. The following are some examples of such activities.

Four Walls

Preparation: Select a fill-in-the-blank phrase (e.g., "If I were a form of transportation, I would be a _____") along with four possible choices (e.g., car, boat, airplane, horse). Post a visual of one of the choices in each corner of the room.

Duration: 5–10 minutes

Materials required: Visuals of fill-in-the-blank selected choices, pencils or pens, scrap paper

Steps:

1. List the four possible fill-in-the-blank choices for staff.

2. Staff members write their choices down on pieces of scrap paper.

3. Staff members move to the corner of the room that exhibits the visual of their choice.

4. Once in their corners, participants break into pairs.

5. In their pairs, participants take turns explaining why they made their choices to each other.

6. Randomly select participants to share their partners' reasons for selecting their choice.

Up-Pair-Share

Preparation: Select a discussion question (e.g., "What was the best workshop you ever attended?").

Duration: 5–10 minutes

Materials required: None

Steps:

1. Ask participants to stand and take a certain number of steps in any direction of the room.

2. Ask participants to find the person closest to them and pair up.

3. Announce the discussion question and the amount of time allotted to discuss it.

4. Partners take turns answering the question to one another.

5. When the discussions are over, randomly select participants to share their partners' responses.

Sample topic ideas:

• "What extracurricular activities did you participate in as a student and what effect did they have on you?"

• "What is most rewarding about being a teacher?"

• "If you could witness any historical event, what would it be?"

• "If you could travel anywhere, where would you go?"

Up-Down

Preparation: Select a number of "stand up if . . ." statements to share (e.g., "Stand up if you enjoyed learning about geography as a student.").

Duration: 5–10 minutes

Materials required: None

Steps:

1. Make a "stand up if . . ." statement.

2. Participants to whom the statement applies stand up briefly, then sit back down.

3. Repeat the process.

Sample "stand up if . . ." statements:
Stand up if . . .

• You had a pet as a child.

• You have three or more siblings.

• You thrive on competition.

• You enjoy drawing and painting.

Get in Line

Preparation: Select a statement on which staff members have varying opinions (e.g., "Technology will reduce the number of teachers needed in schools.").

Duration: 5–10 minutes

Materials required: Scrap paper, pens or pencils

Steps:

1. Present the statement or question to participants, along with one possible answer from each extreme of opinion (e.g., "strongly agree" and "strongly disagree"). Ask participants to draw a line on a piece of scrap paper, with the extremes of opinion that you've provided at either end, and then to mark where on the continuum their own opinions would fall.

2. Once participants have recorded their responses, ask them to stand and form a "living" version of the continuum by standing shoulder to shoulder at the front of the room.

3. Participants pair up with whomever is next to them on the continuum and take turns explaining their place on the continuum.

4. Randomly select several staff members to share their partners' responses.

Sample statements:
- "Technology will reduce the number of teachers needed in schools."
- "School administrators should be required to teach."
- "Portfolios are valuable for assessing student learning."

Concentric Circles

Preparation: Select discussion questions to share (e.g., "When you were a student, who was your favorite teacher and why?").

Duration: 10–15 minutes

Materials required: None

Steps:

1. Ask all participants to stand and form a circle.

2. Participants go around the circle clockwise, alternately labeling themselves as either A or B.

3. The As take a giant step forward then turn to face the Bs so that every A is paired with a B.

4. Announce the discussion question.

5. Participants in each A-B pair take turns answering the question and listening to their partners' responses.

6. Randomly select a few participants to share their partners' responses.

7. Ask participants to rotate one person clockwise to form new pairs.

8. Repeat the process, using either the same question or a different one.

Sample questions:
- "If you could be remembered for anything, what would it be and why?"
- "If you could jump into a movie, which one would it be and why?"

Professional Development Activities

Cooperative Reading

Preparation: Make one copy of a short article on teaching for every teacher. (If the article is longer than two pages, you can provide a summary instead.)

Duration: 15–20 minutes, depending on the length of the article

Materials required: Copies of a short article on teaching (or a summary thereof), pencils or pens, paper

Steps:

1. Provide each participant with a copy of the short article on teaching.

2. Ask participants to form pairs.

3. All participants silently read the article.

4. One person from each pair summarizes the contents of the article for the other, who listens carefully and provides feedback on the accuracy and completeness of the summary.

5. Ask all participants to consider how the article relates to what they already know.

6. Partners work together to write a list of three or more implications for their teaching that the article suggests.

7. Participants form new pairs.

8. Partners share their lists with each other and add one item from each other's list to their own.

Jigsaw

Preparation: Select an article on teaching, and then divide it into three equally long sections. Make enough copies of each reading for everyone at the meeting.

Duration: 20–30 minutes, depending on the length of the reading

Materials required: Copies of a selected article or reading, pencils or pens, paper

Steps:

1. Divide participants into groups of three.

2. Within every group, assign a different section of

the article to each member.

3. Inform participants that the goal is for all group members to understand the content of the entire reading.

4. Ask all group members to leave their groups and pair up with someone assigned to the same section.

5. Inform participants that they have two goals: to become experts on their assigned sections, and to plan how to teach their section to the members of their original group.

6. When the pairs have all achieved their goals, ask participants to form new pairs, once again with teachers who've read the same section.

7. Ask participants to review their instructional plans with their new partners.

8. When the new pairs are done with their review, ask participants to return to their original three-person groups.

9. Each member teaches his or her section of the article to the other group members.

10. When the group members have finished, randomly select a few participants to summarize the content of the entire article.

Problem Trade

Preparation: Think of a discussion topic of concern to staff.

Duration: 15–20 minutes

Materials required: Pencils and pens, paper

Steps:

1. Share the discussion topic with staff.

2. Divide participants into groups of three or four.

3. Ask participants to discuss the topic in their groups.

4. Each group writes down a problem that group members have had related to the topic, along with a solution-seeking question.

5. Going clockwise, groups trade their papers.

6. Group members brainstorm potential answers to the question on the papers they've received and write them down.

7. When the time is up, each group returns its answers the group that provided the question.

8. Ask the groups to decide upon and then report the best idea that they received.

Turn to Your Neighbor

Preparation: Select a professional development presentation, such as a video, to show at the meeting.

Duration: Varies depending on the length of the presentation

Material required: Video or other professional development presentation

Steps:

1. After watching the presentation with participants, divide them into pairs.

2. Pose a question related to the presentation.

3. Each participant formulates an individual answer to the question and shares it with his or her partner, who actively listens.

4. Randomly selects a few participants to share their partners' answers.

Give to Receive

Preparation: Select a problem to discuss at the meeting (e.g., how to motivate students).

Duration: 5–15 minutes

Material required: None

Steps:

1. Ask participants to individually list ideas for addressing the discussion topic in class and to stand up when they are done.

2. When all participants are standing, ask them to form pairs and share their ideas.

Study Groups

Teacher study groups can either meet during staff meetings or replace meetings altogether. Working in these groups can help teachers to learn new instructional techniques, research lesson topics, and solve any number of problems related to teaching. To encourage interdependence and accountability, study groups should be composed of two to five staff members, depending on what is being studied. (The participants themselves decide what to study in their groups.)

Steps to Getting Started

1. At a staff meeting, explain to faculty that teacher study groups have the following characteristics:

• They are composed of participants constructing knowledge through research and focused, collegial discourse.

• All group members acknowledge that everyone in the group has a contribution to make.

• Group members commit to using the knowledge acquired in the group to positively affect perspective, policies, and practice in the school or district.

2. Distribute the Study Group Selection Survey (Appendix 1, p. 135) to all in attendance. (Feel free to modify the survey to reflect local needs and available resources.) Explain to the teachers that they are to read all of the choices on the form and indicate at least three topics they would like to further analyze.

3. When you have received all of the completed forms, use the Study Group Organization Chart (Appendix 1, p. 136) to assign teachers to study groups.

4. Distribute relevant books and articles to each study group.

5. Create folders for each study group that include enough copies of the Study Group Log (Appendix 1, p. 137) for each scheduled study group meeting. Explain that each group is to fill out a log at each meeting.

6. Have all teachers move into their assigned groups. If the group members do not already know one another, have them introduce themselves through an icebreaker activity.

7. Share your expectations with the groups. (Examples: All assignments are to be completed prior to group meetings; everyone will actively participate in discussions.)

8. Explain the following study group roles to faculty:

• **The facilitator** encourages contributions from all group members and keeps the group focused on the task at hand.

• **The recorder** takes notes on the group's discussions.

• **The reporter** reports out the group's achievements at the end of each meeting.

• **The materials manager** returns the study group folder and any other materials back to their places at the end of the meeting.

9. Ask each group to develop a schedule for reading assignments and attach a Study Group Reading Schedule form (Appendix 1, p. 138) to the front cover of its group folder.

Steps for Conducting Study Group Meetings

1. Teachers move into their assigned groups.

2. The materials manager for each group obtains the group folder.

3. The recorder fills in the appropriate sections of the group log.

4. Group members discuss their assigned reading. As they do this, the recorder completes the remainder of the log while still participating in the discussion, and the facilitator ensures that everyone in the group is focused and involved.

5. During the discussions, be sure to circulate among the groups and join in as appropriate.

6. When the time has expired, direct the reporter from each group to share the group's achievements. After each group shares, members of other groups can ask for clarification or elaboration.

7. After all of the groups have shared, facilitate a whole-group discussion on what everybody learned.

8. At the end of the meeting, the facilitators remind their study groups of the next meeting date and reading assignment and the materials manager returns the group's folder to the assigned location.

Problem-Solving Strategies

The secret to finding effective solutions is knowing exactly what you're trying to solve. All too often, the solutions put in place in schools have little effect on the problem they're meant to address. The Problem Interrogation strategy can be used to isolate the root cause of most problems. Once this root cause has been established, the Brainstorming and Affinity strategies can be used to address it.

Problem Interrogation

Preparation: Develop a "problem statement" that is objective and factual and does not imply a solution (e.g., "Approximately 30 percent of our 5th graders and 50 percent of our 6th graders were sent to the office with a discipline referral this year.").

Duration: 10–20 minutes

Materials required: None

Steps:

1. Ask why the problem occurs and identify a potential cause.

Example:

Q: Why did we have so many discipline referrals in 5th and 6th grades this year?

A: Because many students don't know how to act appropriately.

2. Having identified a second problem in the cause of the first, repeat the process.

Example:

Q: Why did many students not know how to act appropriately?

A: Because they don't know the school rules.

3. Continue this pattern of questioning until you arrive at an actionable statement.

Example:

Q: Why do many students not know the school rules?

A: Because we haven't explained and enforced the school rules consistently.

Q: Why haven't we explained and enforced the school rules consistently?

A: Because we haven't agreed on a common set of behavioral expectations.

Q: Why haven't we agreed upon a common set of expectations?

A: Because we have many new 5th and 6th grade teachers who aren't aware of our expectations.

Action: *Brainstorm a common set of expectations.*

Brainstorming

Preparation: Determine a topic (e.g., "common behavior expectations for 5th and 6th grade students") and a time frame or goal.

Duration: Varies

Materials required: Chart paper, marker

Steps:

1. Review the following brainstorming guidelines:
   • Quantity of ideas is more important than quality.
   • There is to be no criticism of any ideas.
   • Building on others' ideas is encouraged.

2. Inform participants of the topic and time frame.

3. Provide one minute of silent thinking time.

4. Select a volunteer to stand by the chart paper with a marker, ready to record ideas.

5. Begin brainstorming. Those with ideas to share must raise their hands and wait for you to call on them. As ideas are called out, the recorder writes them down on the chart paper.

6. The process continues until the time has expired or the goal has been met.

Affinity

Preparation: Select a problem question to discuss.

Materials required: Sticky notes, pencils or pens

Duration: 15–20 minutes

Steps:

1. Divide participants into groups of six to eight.

2. Announce the problem question (e.g., "What should our common behavioral expectations be?")

3. Each participant writes an idea on a sticky note.

4. Going clockwise, each participant shares his or her idea with the group and places the sticky note on the wall.

5. Once all of the participants have shared their ideas, the groups work to cluster similar ideas together.

6. Group members decide upon names for each idea cluster.

7. Groups rotate around the room, examining the other groups' idea clusters.

Decision Making

The decision-making process affords staff members the opportunity to express their ideas and opinions. When groups have to make decisions, conflicts among team members are inevitable. Because decision-making requires a choice among alternative courses of action, the process is by its very nature controversial; indeed, an absence of controversy may signal apathy, disinterest, or alienation among group members. The following strategies can help promote effective decision making in faculty meetings.

Talking Tokens

Preparation: Select a discussion topic.

Duration: 10–15 minutes

Materials required: Colored tokens

Steps:

1. Divide attendees into teams of three or four and distribute a set of colored tokens to each participant, making sure that no two team members have the same color.

2. Share the topic for discussion with the teams.

3. Discussion proceeds according to the following rule: before team members can speak, they must place one of their tokens in the center of the table, except for when they are requested to answer a direct question from another team member.

4. Once all of a staff member's tokens are gone, he or she may not speak until everyone else is also out of tokens.

5. When all of the tokens are in the center of the table, they are redistributed and the process is repeated.

Dot Voting

Preparation: Select a number of options for teachers to vote on, and display them in the meeting room.

Duration: 5–15 minutes

Materials required: Four colored dots per participant

Process: Ask staff members to place their dots on the alternatives they favor. They may spend all of their dots on one idea or spread them out among different alternatives. The idea with the most votes wins.

Rank and Sum

Preparation: Select a number of options for staff members to discuss.

Duration: 15–20 minutes

Steps:

1. Divide participants into groups of three or four.

2. Provide each participant with a list of alternatives to consider.

3. Direct each participant to rank the alternatives in order of preference.

4. Add up all the rankings for each alternative.

5. Select one representative from each team to post the team's totals.

6. Add up the scores for each team.

7. The alternative with the highest score is selected.

Decision-Making Triads

Preparation: None

Duration: 25–30 minutes

Materials required: Pencils or pens

Steps:

1. An advisory committee presents its view of the problem and a recommended solution.

2. Divide staff members into groups of three. Each triad decides whether to accept or modify the committee's recommendation and writes out its reason for the decision.

3. Triads report out their decisions and rationale to staff.

4. Whole-group discussion ensues.

5. An initial vote is conducted to identify the top three alternatives, with each staff member getting three votes.

6. A final vote is conducted to determine which alternative the staff will adopt, with each staff member getting one vote.

7. Triads re-form, commit publicly to supporting the decision, and clarify their responsibilities in implementing the decision.

Concluding Meetings on a Positive Note

At the end of each faculty meeting, staff members should return to their base groups, where they should summarize the meeting, discuss what actions to take, and celebrate staff members' efforts. Team celebrations will increase teachers' commitment to their work. There are few things more motivating then having colleagues affirm your contributions to a school. Celebrations create positive interactions and provide concrete evidence that people care about one another. Within schools, it is genuine acts of caring that draw people together and move organizations forward. Love of teaching, students, and colleagues is what inspires many staff members to commit more of their energy to their jobs. Concluding your faculty meetings with short team-based opportunities to celebrate and affirm each other's efforts will give your staff the courage to continue in times of turmoil and stress.

Meeting Minutes

Many faculty meetings will result in action items for participants to complete. As most experienced administrators can attest, it is unwise to assume that all attendees will take their assignments to heart and remember the details of their assignments. Meeting minutes serve as a record of the topics addressed, decisions reached, and responsibilities assigned at the meeting, and are especially helpful to staff members who could not attend the meeting. The recorder should type up the minutes and provide them to you within 24 hours of the meeting ending. Once you've reviewed the minutes for accuracy, distribute them to all staff no later than 48 hours after the meeting has finished, mak-

ing sure to retain a copy for yourself. An example of meeting minutes appears in Figure 2.1.

2.1 Sample Meeting Minutes

Members in Attendance: Principal Winters, E. Greene, H. Sharpe, M. DeShanes, J. O'Brien, K. Vafiadis, M. Kozar, K. Karrenbauer, M. Grazer, J. Bauman, C. Lefebrve, K. Koot, M. DeBenedictis, H. Hampson, T. Withka.

Members Absent: D. Gibson, R. Semko

Topics:

• *Staff development:* Several possible topics were discussed for the upcoming inservice day. The decision was made to have a guest speak on methods of working with students who lack social skills in the morning, with discussion time in the afternoon. Principal Winters will contact a speaker and update the faculty at the next meeting.

• *Adequate yearly progress:* Principal Winters and Ms. Greene presented the school's results on the standardized test. Overall progress has been demonstrated in math and science, but we continue to have a limited number of students meeting the advanced proficiency requirements. Principal Winters suggested forming a subcommittee to further study this idea.

Concerns: The problem of parents entering the building without visitor's passes was brought up. It was suggested that custodians stand by the two side doors so that they can direct parents to the front of the building. The staff member supervising bus duty would then direct parents to the office for a visitor's pass.

3

Dealing with Difficult Situations

In the middle of difficulty lies opportunity.
—Albert Einstein

During a crisis or tragedy, your role as a leader is magnified. Consider the following scenario:

Mr. Simmons listened to the voice on the other end of the line in disbelief: a popular, highly respected physical education teacher had been killed in a car crash on his way home from work that day.

After a few minutes of feeling strangely disconnected from reality, Mr. Simmons reminded himself of the need to call the superintendent, Mr. Kline. When reached, Mr. Kline reminded Mr. Simmons that according to the district's crisis management plan, he needed to activate the phone chain and hold an emergency staff meeting early the next morning.

What was he going to say? How would staff react to the news? Mr. Simmons felt suddenly nauseated. He rummaged through his desk for the district's crisis protocol manual. In the section on emergencies of this kind, step two read, *Hold a full staff meeting as soon as possible after the event.* That was all; no additional details about the nature or content of this meeting were provided.

It occurred to Mr. Simmons that this would be a long and difficult evening: he had to plan a meeting for the morning while still dealing with the shock of the event himself.

Determining the Need for an Emergency Meeting

Most districts have comprehensive crisis management plans that mandate sharing the nature of a sudden, unexpected event with staff. Observe your school community's response to the crisis and use your judgment to determine if an emergency meeting is required. If you are unsure about the need for a meeting, ask yourself the following questions:

- Does the crisis affect the majority of the school community?
- Is it possible for the crisis to get worse?
- Does the response to the crisis require outside resources?
- Does the situation surrounding the crisis risk spinning out of control?
- Is the crisis creating or likely to create rumors and hysteria?

If the answer to any of these questions is yes, then an emergency meeting is advisable.

Emergency Staff Meeting Agenda Template

Because it can be hard to think clearly during a crisis, it's a good idea to have a meeting agenda template ready to meet the circumstances, such as the one in Figure 3.1.

3.1 Emergency Staff Meeting Agenda Template

1. Review the events that have occurred. Provide factual information and avoid speculation.

2. Update staff on the school and community response to the crisis or tragedy so far.

3. Outline any unfamiliar facets of the crisis management plan (e.g., the use of counseling support rooms for students and staff).

4. Review any changes to the school schedule and any other upcoming procedural accommodations.

5. Distribute and review notification announcements. Discuss plans for notifying parents and students.

6. Review school or district policies relating to the media. Emphasize that all media inquiries should be referred to a school or district spokesperson. Stress the importance of notifying the administration if members of the media show up at the school.

7. Allow staff the opportunity to ask questions and voice concerns. If someone is so stricken by the event that he or she has trouble discussing it, arrange for an assistant to notify that teacher's students.

8. Conclude the meeting by scheduling a follow-up meeting within 24 hours.

Follow-Up Meetings

Use follow-up meetings to provide staff with any new information, solicit feedback on handling of the crisis or tragedy, and offer assistance where needed. When the crisis or tragedy has subsided, hold a final meeting to review how it was handled and make necessary changes to the crisis management plan.

Difficult Meeting Participants

Some people lack either the interpersonal skills or the desire to work effectively in a large group setting; others bring personal issues to meetings with them that negatively influence their attitudes and actions. To ensure that difficult participants do not disrupt your meeting, adhere to the following guidelines:

- **Contain digression.** Do not permit drawn-out personal examples or discussions that are irrelevant to the task at hand. Remind staff members politely that discussion topics should relate to the agenda and should be relevant to most in attendance.
- **Act as a gatekeeper.** It may be necessary at times to coax opinions from less-assertive staff members and to ask those who are dominating discussions to let others participate.
- **Manage disagreements.** You must learn to recognize tension when it builds in a group and respond to it immediately. One of the most useful strategies is to repeat the meeting's ground rules and remind staff that criticism should pertain to ideas, not people.

When approaching a difficult meeting participant to discuss his or her behavior, your first step should be to arrange for a private, one-on-one conversation.

The following scenarios illustrate the appropriate way of addressing five common types of difficult participants.

The Naysayer

On his way to work in the morning, Mr. Johnson finds himself thinking about the staff meeting scheduled for after school. Mr. Walters, a math teacher, is very difficult at meetings. Whenever someone proposes a solution to a problem, he counters with reasons why the suggestion won't work. Mr. Johnson has noticed that Mr. Walters's actions dissuade other staff members from offering contributions, and that his colleagues are clearly annoyed by him. This situation is especially frustrating to Mr. Johnson because he knows that Mr. Walters has a wealth of knowledge and experience that is not being expressed productively.

Mr. Walters is an example of a naysayer: someone who reflexively disagrees with the suggestions of others. To work more effectively with naysayers, follow these suggestions:

- Ask the naysayer what alternatives he or she would propose.
- Ask the group for opinions on the naysayer's comments.
- Ask the naysayer, "What would have to change for the proposed solution to work?" Do not accept "It won't work" as a response.

The Aggressor

Mr. Johnson has come to the conclusion that most staff members are intimidated by Ms. Marrone. Whenever they offer opinions that differ from hers, she either shoots them dirty looks or insults them. At the last meeting, she even called one of Mr. Johnson's ideas "childish" and "simplistic," which is when he lost his temper and berated Ms. Marrone for five minutes. When the meeting fell into an awkward silence, Mr. Johnson ended the meeting. Although he felt a bit better after letting his feelings be known, he knew that he still did not have an acceptable long-term strategy for dealing with Ms. Marrone.

Ms. Marrone is an example of an aggressor: someone who expresses disagreement inappropriately. To work more effectively with aggressors, follow these suggestions:

• Remind the aggressor to limit comments to ideas rather than people.

• Refer the aggressor to the staff's agreed-upon norms of behavior for meetings.

• Ask other participants if they agree with the aggressor's statements.

• If the aggressor's comment is not directed at an individual, ignore it until the break, when you can speak privately.

• If the statement is made directly to you, be professional and respectful. Acknowledge that there are different ways to think about any given topic. Avoid becoming defensive or getting drawn into an argument.

The Dominator

Mrs. Adams, a 6th grade teacher, was repeating her opinion of the new dress code for the third time in as many meetings. Mr. Johnson noticed that when she would raise her hand to speak, her coworkers would roll their eyes or start working on unrelated items.

Mrs. Adams is an example of a dominator: someone who dominates discussions with redundant or unnecessarily long responses. To work more effectively with dominators, follow these suggestions:

• Break eye contact with the dominator and call on someone else by name to provide a suggestion.

• Impose a time limit on all staff members' responses.

• When the dominator pauses for breath, take the opportunity to ask for someone else's opinion.

• Hold your hand up, palm facing outward.

• Post a flip chart on the wall at the beginning of every meeting and label it "Parking Lot." Put sticky notes in easily accessible locations. When a participant exhibits the characteristics of a dominator, write down his or her comment on the sticky note and place it on the flip chart. At the end of the meeting, review the comments with the dominator.

The Attention Seeker

Mr. Stanton would often interject humor at meetings. At first Mr. Johnson thought his comments were funny, but they were starting to grate on his nerves. Other staff members also seemed annoyed, especially when Mr. Stanton would crack jokes during discussions of sober topics.

Mr. Stanton is an example of an attention seeker: someone who feels the need to be the focal point at meetings. To work more effectively with attention seekers, follow these suggestions:

• Ask attention seekers to help with tasks such as demonstrations, thus using their desire for attention to your advantage.

• If the attention-seeking behavior is not disruptive, ignore it (e.g., by turning your back to the attention seeker).

The Avoider

It never fails: Mr. Martin and Mrs. Lee are late to every staff meeting. When they do arrive, they engage in side conversations with one another and don't participate in the larger discussion. Principal Johnson has heard rumblings of resentment among staff about the duo's constant tardiness, and notices their apathy rubbing off on their coworkers.

Mr. Martin and Mrs. Lee are examples of avoiders: those who cannot or will not focus at meetings. To work more effectively with avoiders, follow these suggestions:

• Start meetings on time and with engaging activities.
• Have staff members catch up with you after the meeting or during breaks if they need to be informed of what they've missed.

• Arrange the physical environment so that you can make eye contact with all staff members at all times.
• When avoiders engage in side conversations, walk toward them casually while continuing to lead the meeting, then stand near them until they cease talking.
• When a staff member appears reluctant to participate in a large group activity, address him or her directly.

As a last resort, you may need to ask a difficult staff member to leave a meeting. The best way to do so is to call for a break and speak with the disruptive person in private.

4 | Evaluating and Improving Faculty Meetings

A leader takes people where they want to go. A great leader takes people where they ought to be.
— Abraham Lincoln

Evaluating Meetings

You should regularly assess the effectiveness of your meetings using the Faculty Meeting Rating Survey (Appendix 1, p. 139).

Implementing a One-Year Improvement Plan

Use the following one-year plan to bridge the gap between the status quo and your vision for efficient meetings. (If colleagues are embarking on the plan as well, get together with them regularly to review progress, discuss problems, and develop solutions. Working with peers will go a long way toward helping sustain momentum along your journey.)

Two or More Weeks Prior to Implementation

- Send a memo communicating a change in faculty meetings to staff.
- Examine the physical environment of the meeting room. Make changes to the room as required and feasible.
- Obtain any necessary materials required to facilitate the meetings.
- Create faculty base teams.

Two Days Prior to Implementation

• Determine your meeting objectives (professional development, staff building, problem solving, decision making).
• Create an agenda for the meeting that is based on your objectives. Distribute the agenda at least 24 hours in advance of the meeting.
• Arrange seats as desired.
• Arrange for refreshments.
• Disseminate the meeting agenda.
• Secure all meeting supplies. Check to make sure all of the audiovisual aids are in working order.

First Meeting (Approx. 45 minutes)

• Arrive early and greet staff members as they arrive.
• Start the meeting on time. Have staff members form into base teams and conduct a team-building activity.
• Explain and assign meeting roles.
• Complete the meeting agreements activity.
• Have staff members complete a "check-out" in their base teams. End the meeting on time.

Post-Meeting

Distribute the meeting minutes within 48 hours of the meeting. Include a copy of the faculty meeting agreements. (If you wish, turn these agreements into displays for future meetings.)

Repeat the above process for subsequent meetings.

Every Six to Eight Meetings

• Have staff members complete the Faculty Meeting Survey. Review the results and make the changes.
• Form new faculty meeting base teams.

As Necessary

• Review the preceding chapter for ideas on how to deal with difficult situations.
• Implement suggestions and evaluate results.
• Brainstorm ideas with colleagues.
• Arrange for a colleague to observe your faculty meeting. Meet afterward to review any possible areas for improvement.

Although many teachers and principals dread faculty meetings, they are occasions that beg to be used productively. By following the suggestions in this section, you can help teachers develop the skills necessary to meet the challenges of increased accountability. Your meetings will serve as valuable professional development tools rather than "45-minute memos."

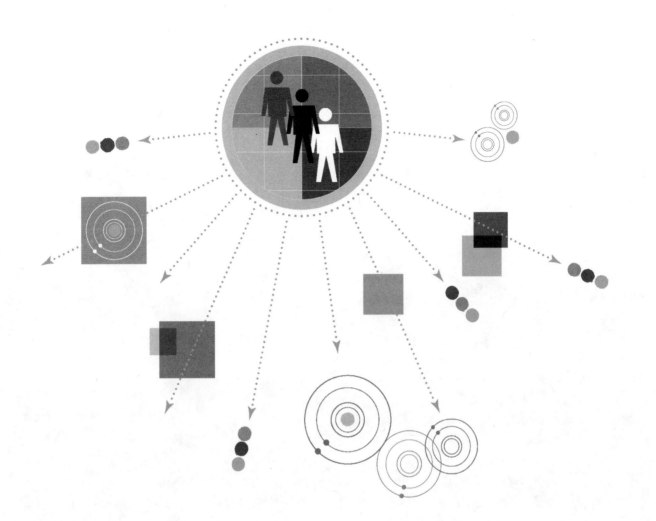

Section 2

Inclusion Teaching Teams

Introduction

Early in my career as a special education teacher, I realized that, despite my best efforts, students in my pullout resource center classes were not closing the achievement gap with their peers. At first I thought this had to do with my teaching skills and experience, but as time went by, I realized that the gap was more the norm than the exception. Following this realization, I began to examine the structural elements of instructional models for special education, which eventually led me to conclude that pullout models are ineffective for meeting the academic and social needs of most students with learning disabilities. Both the research and my discussions with other special educators convinced me that collaborative teaching teams in inclusion classrooms offer a more promising approach.

As a teacher, I worked for several years to help initiate such teaching teams in a middle school. Being new to this model of instruction, I sought out all of the resources I could find. With the help of workshops, videos, textbooks, and other materials, the teaching teams at our school resulted in improved academic and social outcomes for many students.

Naturally, upon becoming the director of student services in a different school district, I wanted to replicate this success. In preparing to overhaul a special education program with a strong emphasis on the pullout model, I once again sought out materials to guide me. This time, I was astonished to find a lack of appropriate resources. Although many materials were available for teachers, few existed for administrators, and those that did were not adequate.

Discouraged but not defeated, I persisted in my efforts. It was a difficult road with many detours and potholes along the way, but I never lost faith, and eventually an inclusion teaching team program was established for the district. The contents of this section are the result of this journey. It is my sincere hope that the ideas and materials contained within these pages will help you to implement and support inclusion teaching teams.

May your journey be filled with fewer detours and potholes than mine. Happy travels!

5

Understanding Inclusion Teaching Teams

If a person does not know to which port he is sailing,
no wind is favorable.

—Seneca

Sitting in her office, Mrs. Adams wondered how things had come to this point.

Mrs. Johnson, a third-year special education teacher, had just handed in her letter of resignation. This wasn't completely unexpected, as she had come to Mrs. Adams in tears on several occasions, expressing her frustration with collaborative teaching relationships. As she explained it, she was being asked to teach alongside four different teachers in four different subject areas, with no common planning time. Although she wanted to help her students and colleagues, Mrs. Johnson felt forced into the role of instructional assistant. "This is not why I went to college," she'd say. She was also tired of hearing her colleagues complain about how easy she had it—how lucky she was not to have a homeroom, for instance, or 100 papers to grade at any given time.

Mrs. Johnson had come to resent her colleagues, and tended to feel like a guest in the classroom. As she said to Mrs. Adams, "My colleagues always refer to the classroom as theirs—but to the students with disabilities as mine."

Mrs. Adams reflected on Mrs. Johnson's situation and wondered what she might have done to prevent it. When she first became a principal, collaborative teaching models did not even exist. Not only had she never taught collaboratively, but she had never had any graduate coursework or training to prepare her to do so. Yet she knew that collaborative teaching was not going away, especially in light of a federal mandate to educate students with disabilities in the least-restrictive environments. Though she did not like to admit it, Mrs. Adams secretly yearned for the old days of self-contained classrooms and resource centers. Sometimes she wondered why schools switched to collaborative teaching anyway.

Background

According to Lipsky and Gartner (1995), 891 districts representing all 50 states reported having inclusion programs in their schools. These districts reported that collaborative teaching was more common than any other model for inclusive instruction; more recently, Weiss and Lloyd (2002) reaffirmed this assessment. It appears that Mrs. Adams's hunch was correct: collaborative teaching seems here to stay in inclusion classrooms. Typically in such situations, two teachers—one for students with disabilities and one for general education students—work together to develop a differentiated curriculum that meets the needs of the whole class. These two teachers collaborate on planning and presenting lessons, evaluating student work, and managing the classroom.

The Legal Basis for Collaborative Teaching

The Individuals with Disabilities Education Improvement Act of 2004 (IDEIA) ensures access to free and appropriate education for students with disabilities. Although the law does not specifically mandate teaching teams in inclusion classrooms, it does require districts to place students with disabilities in the "least-restrictive environment" (LRE). The "supplementary aids and services" referred to in the following IDEIA language may be interpreted as including collaborative instruction:

> To the maximum extent appropriate, children with disabilities, including children in public or private institutions or other care facilities, are educated with children that are not disabled . . . special classes, separate schooling, or other removal of children with disabilities from the regular education environment occurs only when the nature and severity of the disability is such that education in regular classes with the use of supplementary aids and services cannot be achieved satisfactorily.

The Individualized Education Planning Team

The decision as to what constitutes an LRE for each special education student is up to that student's individualized education program (IEP) team. At a minimum, the IEP team must include

- The student's parents or guardians.
- Someone who can interpret the results of the completed evaluations.
- A general education teacher.
- A special education teacher.
- A representative of the school district (frequently, but not always, the school principal).

The primary purpose of the IEP team is to consider what setting or combination of settings is most appropriate for meeting the student's identified needs. Although the law requires a continuum of placement alternatives, it is clear that placement in a general education classroom with appropriate supports and services is favored. The school administration will not be able to overrule the team's decision in this regard, but it will have a major influence on how collaborative instruction is implemented.

Research

The following are some examples of findings on inclusion teaching teams that are drawn from the research base:

➤ Fishbaugh and Gum (1994) note that when one Montana school district implemented inclusion programs for students with disabilities in some of its elementary schools, it resulted in two to three years of academic improvement for several of the students.

➤ An analysis of inclusion programs in Minnesota concluded that they helped students with mild disabilities to perform better on reading assessments (Deno, Maruyana, Espin, & Cohen, 1990).

➤ In a 1992 study, Jenkins and colleagues found that students in an inclusion program did significantly better on vocabulary, total reading, and language skills assessments than did students in schools with pullout programs.

➤ England (1996) found that test scores in collaboratively taught classrooms remained steady in the first year of one Missouri district's inclusion program, whereas the scores in the district's pullout program did not.

➤ Waldron and McLeskey (1998) examined the effects of one inclusion program on the reading and math achievement of students with disabilities and found that the students did better than did their counterparts in resource center classrooms. In addition, Waldron and McLeskey found that students with mild learning disabilities who were in inclusion programs showed progress comparable to that of their general education peers.

➤ Rea, McLaughlin, and Walther-Thomas (2002) found that students in inclusion classrooms earned higher grades, did better on standardized tests, and attended school more frequently than did their peers in pullout programs.

➤ In a study of 43 classrooms in 14 schools, Cole and Meyer (1991) found that students in inclusion classrooms did better on assessments of social competence than did students in pullout programs.

➤ Saint-Laurent and Lessard (1991) found that teachers of inclusion classrooms reported more significant behavioral improvement among students with disabilities than did teachers of pullout programs.

➤ Hunt and Farron-Davis (1992) determined that students with severe disabilities placed in inclusion programs were subject to IEPs with more references to best practices than were students in pullout programs. Students in inclusion classrooms were also less likely to be engaged in isolated activities.

➤ Hunt, Farron-Davis, Beckstead, Curtis, and Goetz (1994) found significant differences between students in inclusion classrooms and those in pullout programs in the following areas: level of engagement in school activities, type of activities engaged in, type and level of participation in integrated school environments, and level of social engagement with peers and adults.

➤ Hunt, Soto, Maier, and Doering (2003) studied the effect of an inclusion teaching team on six students and found that, when implemented consistently, the model was associated with increased academic skills, engagement in classroom activities, interactions with peers, and student-initiated interactions.

➤ Odom, DeKlyen, and Jenkins (1984) found no difference between general education students in inclusion and noninclusion classrooms on cognitive, linguistic, and social development measures.

➤ After analyzing test results and report cards in a rural Minnesota elementary school, Sharpe, York, and Knight (1994) found no significant academic or behavioral changes among general education students educated alongside peers with disabilities.

➤ In a study of cooperative learning groups, Hunt, Staub, Alwell, and Goetz (1994) concluded that general education students who worked with peers who had severe disabilities saw no adverse effect on their level of academic achievement.

➤ Hollowood, Salisbury, Rainforth, and Palombaro (1995) found that instructional time for general education students is not adversely affected by the presence of students with severe disabilities in the classroom.

➤ Helmstetter, Peck, and Giangreco (1994) surveyed 166 Washington state high school students who had been in inclusion classrooms and found that they did not believe inclusion caused them to miss out on other valuable educational experiences.

➤ In a yearlong ethnographic study, Murray-Seegert (1989) concluded that general education students become more tolerant of others as they become more aware of their peers' needs.

➤ Helmstetter and colleagues (1994) found that inclusion helps general education students develop positive attitudes towards classmates with disabilities.

➤ According to Staub and Peck (1995), inclusion programs help general education elementary students to more effectively communicate with peers who have special needs and to be more supportive of them in their daily interactions. The authors also found that many general education students become more strongly committed to moral and ethical principles as a result of interacting with special education classmates.

➤ Helmstetter and colleagues (1994) and Staub, Schwartz, Gallucci, and Peck (1994) note that inclusion programs seem to have a positive effect on relationships among students, and Fryxell and Kennedy (1995) found this to be just as true for students with severe disabilities.

➤ In a study of middle school students with severe disabilities, Kennedy, Shakla, and Fryxell (1997) found that those in an inclusion classroom interacted more frequently with general education peers, provided and received more social support, and had larger, more durable networks of general education classmates than did students in a pull-out program.

➤ Although Giangreco, Dennis, Cloninger, Edelman, and Schattman (1993) found that most teachers of inclusion classrooms initially react negatively to teaching a mixed group, they also found that 17 of the 19 teachers they studied indicated that, after teaching one student with severe disabilities for a year, they were willing to teach another the following year.

➤ In a survey of 680 teachers and administrators in 32 schools, Villa, Thousand, Meyers, and Nevin (1996) found that educators believe inclusion helps change their attitudes and job responsibilities for the better. The study also found that levels of administrative support and collaboration were powerful predictors of positive attitudes toward full inclusion.

➤ Praisner (2003) conducted a survey of 408 elementary school principals and found that roughly one in five had positive attitudes toward inclusion (the rest were uncertain). Principals with more positive attitudes were more likely to place students in less restrictive settings. Survey results lead Praisner to emphasize inclusion practices that allow principals to work with all types of students with disabilities, and to recommend more specific training for principals in special education instruction.

Creating a School Culture That Supports Inclusion Teaching Teams

It was late August, and Mr. James was busy putting the final touches on the school's master schedule. Just when he was almost finished, he received a call from Ms. Jackson, who was a 4th grade teacher in her sixth year of teaching at the school. After exchanging the usual pleasantries, Ms. Jackson got to the point.

"Mr. James," she began, "there is a rumor going around that you have assigned me the inclusion class this year. You know that I love all of my students and I work really hard, but I just don't think I can teach those kids. I haven't had any experience or training working with disabled children. It isn't true that you assigned me to teach that class, is it?"

Although it *was* true that Mr. James had assigned Ms. Jackson to the inclusion class, he valued Ms. Jackson as a teacher and wanted to keep her happy, so he decided to tell her it was *not* true, reasoning that he could assign a recently hired 4th grade teacher to the class instead; this person was excited to have been hired, and probably would not complain.

Contrast Mr. James's response with Mrs. Sharpe's. One day, Mrs. Sharpe, also a principal, received a message from her secretary that Ms. Williams had called. Ms. Williams was a 3rd grade teacher with five years of experience at the school. Mrs. Sharpe decided to return the call before going to a meeting at the central office. Ms. Williams did not bother with the usual pleasantries, choosing instead to get right to the point.

"I received my class assignment, and it shows that I am teaching with Mrs. Rose [the special education teacher]. I want to know if I am teaching one of those classes with all the special education kids. If so, that is unacceptable and I want it changed immediately. I didn't come to this district to teach those kids."

While listening patiently and keeping her cool, Mrs. Sharpe steadfastly conveyed her unwillingness to change Ms. Williams's assignment. She communicated her belief that Ms. Williams would find coteaching to be a positive experience. Despite Ms. Williams's intimations that she would look for another job if she were not reassigned, Mrs. Sharpe expressed her conviction that coteaching was not optional at the school.

Here we have two principals faced with a decision related to collaborative teaching. Each chose a course of action that communicates a strong message: whereas Mr. James's actions reflect a belief that coteaching is a burden to be thrust upon those least likely to object, Mrs. Sharpe's actions reflect a belief that it is a nonnegotiable opportunity for professional growth.

Deficit Versus Competence Orientation

Because language and behaviors influence the way that teaching teams are perceived, educators should avoid a deficit orientation—that is, words and actions that emphasize what students *cannot* do—as this prevents teachers from addressing student strengths. On the other hand, a competence orientation—words and actions that emphasize what students *can* do—help create a climate in which all students' skills, interests, and abilities

can emerge. Instead of ranking and comparing students, teachers focus on understanding them as individuals and providing adapted learning environments that support the integration, participation, and growth of all students.

To demonstrate a competence orientation, educators should

- Focus on the individual rather than on the disability (e.g., *students with disabilities* rather than *handicapped students*).
- Expect all students to participate academically and socially. When students are struggling to complete an assignment or are not participating, they should be encouraged and assisted. Educators must convey high expectations for all students through determination and persistence.
- Act promptly and decisively when they encounter behavior that is inappropriate and hurtful to others. A firm response to put-downs models acceptance of individual differences.
- Correct teacher and student misperceptions of "fairness" regarding the accommodations provided to students with disabilities. Fairness does not entail giving everyone the same thing; rather, it entails giving each person what he or she needs to succeed. Until educators come to agreement on this issue, students with disabilities will achieve limited success in collaboratively taught classrooms.
- Speak directly to students rather than to educational assistants or interpreters.
- Provide opportunities for all students to assume age-appropriate positions of leadership.
- Reflect a sense of ownership regarding all students. When a student with a disability

demonstrates problem behavior or difficulty learning, it is appropriate to seek advice and guidance from those with the appropriate expertise; however, educators must be involved in problem-solving and follow-up activities.

• Not allow parents to choose whether or not to have their students in collaboratively taught classrooms. A good educator would no more allow this than allow parents to choose their children's classroom based on race.

Your Role

Although most of the available research supports inclusion, you must ensure that certain conditions are met if the program in your school or district is to succeed. The criteria for effective teaching teams are not discrete and easily identifiable; in fact, they are intertwined and often as hard to untangle as the backlash on a fishing reel. There are also many different ways in which collaborative teaching teams can act effectively—a principle that systems theorists refer to as "equifinality" (Katz & Kahn, 1978). According to this principle, different teams can reach the same outcome under dissimilar conditions and using different means. Even when the task at hand is identical, no single performance strategy will work equally well for all groups.

When teaching teams do not succeed, individual teachers are usually blamed. Such judgments are misplaced: although teachers are critical to the success of any team, they often face significant barriers to effective performance, such as insufficient planning time. Rather than try to manage individual teachers as they attempt to collaborate with each other, you should create the necessary conditions for teaching teams to prosper while also allowing them to develop their own unique styles and strategies. In the next chapter, we'll examine the steps it takes to create these conditions.

6 Creating Inclusion Teaching Teams

Good plans shape good decisions. That's why good planning helps to make elusive dreams come true.
—Lester Bittel

Let us return to Mrs. Johnson, the frustrated special education teacher in the previous chapter. She was being asked to assume a role that did not use her knowledge and skills. Her colleagues did not understand her role, treating her like a guest in "their" classroom. Is it any surprise that she decided to resign? Tragically, Mrs. Johnson will probably leave the school believing that she failed at collaborative teaching, when in fact her efforts never could have led to a high-performing team, because the team had not been properly designed from the beginning. To set the stage for an effective inclusion teacher team, the educational leader must

- Set the parameters of the team's task.
- Select the appropriate team members.
- Obtain the necessary material resources.
- Ensure an appropriate class composition.

Setting the Parameters of the Team's Task

Teaching teams are what Hackman (2002) calls self-managing: although the educational leader is responsible for their context and design, the teachers themselves are responsible for their performance. As Hackman notes, it is virtually impossible for a team to manage its own affairs competently without someone in authority establishing a direction for the team's work, as such direction allows teams to align specific strategies with ultimate goals.

Your challenge is to clearly specify a team's expected outcomes without specifying the means to achieve them. Direction that is unclear or highly abstract (such as with most school mission statements) wastes members' time and encourages needless conflict as team members try to figure out what exactly they are expected to do. For example, if you were to direct a team to "facilitate students' growth toward their full potential," would the members even know where to start? Does "potential" refer to academic potential, social potential, or both? What is meant by "facilitate"? How can someone's "full potential" possibly be determined? On the other hand, if you were to specify every detail of what should be accomplished, team members may have a diminished sense of ownership toward their work.

A team's goals must be attainable without being uninteresting. There are no clear-cut rules for determining the most appropriate level of challenge, but you should bear in mind the team members' capabilities: different teams may require different goals based upon their knowledge, skill, and experience.

Selecting the Appropriate Team Members

Picture the following scenario: near the end of the school year, a special education teacher and a general education teacher approach you and volunteer to teach an inclusion class together. The teachers are friends outside of school and have very similar teaching styles and philosophies. Pleased that the teachers have volunteered, you assign them to teach a class together in the next school year. However, at the end of the next school year, the teachers' students have made minimal progress and the teachers are no longer on good terms. How could this have happened?

Heterogeneity Versus Homogeneity

Teachers who gravitate toward working with one another tend to have a lot in common. Although they may get along well as a result, they will usually lack the full complement of knowledge and skills to perform effectively (or even to learn from one another). More heterogeneous groups can have trouble as well, especially as they struggle to determine the best way to work together, but they are still likely to come up with more creative strategies and solutions than are homogeneous teams. The ideal teaching team, then, strikes the right balance between homogeneity and heterogeneity.

Support Teams

Teaching teams consist of the teachers directly responsible for all of the teaching responsibilities for all of the students assigned to a classroom. In an inclusion classroom, this usually means a general education teacher, a special education teacher, and, occasionally, one or more paraprofessionals. These are the individuals who work together daily or almost daily to plan, implement, and evaluate their students' lessons. In addition to the teaching team, however, you should also ensure that a support team is in place. Support teams consist of staff members who work with the students less frequently than does the teaching team, such as psychologists, nurses, and occupational or physical therapists. The larger the teaching and support teams, the more difficult it becomes to coordinate actions and communicate effectively, so you should strive to keep both teams as small as possible.

Membership Stability

Teaching teams with stable membership perform better over time than do teams with revolving membership. There are three main reasons for this:

1. The familiarity that develops among members of stable groups allows them to focus on working together rather than waste time getting acquainted.
2. Stable group members get to know one another's skills over time, making them better able to divide up work according to each other's talents.
3. Stable group members are likely to develop a shared commitment to the team and to caring for one another.

Some teachers are just not cut out to be members of a team; they may have a great deal to contribute to the academic achievement of their students, but can do so better working alone. When selecting inclusion teaching team members, be sure to choose those with a certain degree of interpersonal skill.

Teaching Efficacy

Teaching efficacy can be defined as a set of expectations about the effect of instruction on student performance regardless of such variables as student ability and family background (Ashton & Webb, 1986). Because teachers with a high sense of teaching efficacy tend to be more willing to take responsibility for meeting the needs of students with disabilities in their own classrooms, you should select them to join inclusion teaching teams.

The Importance of the Hiring Process

Use the inevitability of staff turnover as an opportunity to hire teachers capable of sustaining long-term systemic change. One effective way to support inclusion teaching teams is to hire teachers who have already developed, or are perceived to have the potential to create, collaborative teaching relationships; it is therefore vitally important that interviewers know enough to properly evaluate each applicant about collaborative teaching. Standard interview questions for this purpose include the following:

• What are some experiences you've had working in a collaborative teaching environment?
• What are some positive and negative experiences you've had working in a collaborative teaching environment?
• How have you handled academic diversity in your teaching experiences?
• What types of instructional strategies have you used to address students' varied approaches to learning?
• How do your instructional objectives address students' varied approaches to learning?

• What kinds of assessments do you use, and how do they help guide your instruction?

• What are some behavioral strategies you've designed for students who have trouble following classroom rules?

• What accommodations have you made for students with special needs? How successful have they been? How did you know?

• What is your process for planning instruction?

• What do you see as the roles and responsibilities of inclusion teaching team members?

Information gleaned during the hiring interview is vital for assessing applicants' qualifications, attitudes, verbal abilities, and potential fit within the organization. Although few novice teachers will have had the opportunity to become superlative team teachers, they are more likely to eventually do so if they possess the appropriate skills and attitudes when they are hired.

Obtaining the Necessary Material Resources

For the purpose of inclusion teaching teams, material resources refer to time and physical space and equipment. Just as the availability of material resources will greatly enhance a team's path toward achieving its objectives, the lack thereof can be disastrous, even for a team that is otherwise well directed, structured, and supported.

Time

Be sure to assess both teacher schedules and common planning time and proactively communicate the benefits of different options to the IEP team.

Schedules

The traditional model of collaborative teaching involves the general education teacher and the special education teacher remaining in the classroom for an entire lesson or school day. For a variety of reasons, this is the ideal model for collaborative teaching. However, there is one major problem with the arrangement: most schools do not have enough special education teachers to collaboratively teach in most general education classrooms, so the few cotaught classrooms become disproportionately filled with students who have special needs.

Consider the following options for addressing a shortage of special education teachers in your school or district. These options enable students with disabilities to access a broader range of general education classes in such situations, and result in an improved ratio of special to general education students. However, they also require special education teachers to miss significant portions of class time, making it hard for them to keep up with class activities. In addition, they risk creating the impression among students that the special education and general education teachers are not equal partners:

➤ **Option 1.** Special education teachers divide their teaching time between two different classes (e.g., between science and social studies) in one or more periods of the school day, based on the activities being conducted and the individual needs of students. One challenge with this option is the disruption to class routine associated with moving in and out of the classroom during instructional time.

➤ **Option 2.** Special education teachers coteach different classes on different days—for example, social studies class on Tuesday and Thursday and science class on Monday, Wednesday, and Friday. The unique advantage to this option is that it provides the teaching team with enough class time to implement strategies effectively; the unique disadvantage is that students with disabilities do not have support in a given class on every day.

➤ **Option 3.** Special education teachers serve as a resource for a team of general education teachers, who identify and schedule essential opportunities for IEP support on a weekly basis. The major advantage to this option is that the special education teacher is present when needed most. This option requires the highest degree of planning and collaboration skills among team members.

➤ **Option 4.** A team of teacher assistants is assigned to a special education teacher and given the responsibility of supporting a caseload of students with disabilities. The special education teacher can meet with a team of general education teachers and determine assignments based on student needs and the assistants' particular competencies. For this option to work, the special education teacher must be skilled at assigning, monitoring, and assisting the paraprofessionals. One advantage of this option is that it takes advantage of the availability of paraprofessionals in the absence of qualified special education teachers—and because paraprofessionals are less costly than teachers, more money can be allocated to support students with disabilities. One disadvantage is that parents often question the ability of paraprofessionals to provide effective support in the absence of direct supervision by the special education teacher.

Common Planning Time

Whichever scheduling option the educational leader chooses, it must include time for collaborative instructional planning, which is at the core of team teaching. One of the major benefits of inclusion teams is that special and general education teachers bring different skills to the table; this is especially helpful during common planning time, when teachers attempt to ensure that their lessons are appropriately differentiated for a heterogeneous class.

If inclusion teaching teams are not provided with common planning time, the special education teacher will usually take a very limited role in the classroom. Unfortunately, the time is often difficult to provide. In such cases, consider the following alternatives:

• Working with the central office to arrange for periodic early release days
• Arranging for teachers to meet during independent work time or recess while teaching assistants or parent volunteers supervise the students
• Allotting time during faculty meetings on alternate weeks for team planning
• Combining classes for a period to free up a teacher's time
• Planning special events on a monthly basis— if the events are operated by nonschool staff, teachers will have free time to meet
• Hiring substitute teachers to rotate among classes
• Using school or district funds to cover compensatory time for teachers

Physical Space and Equipment

Physical Space

Imagine being assigned to move in with another person. What would you do if you did not like the color scheme, furniture, or decorations of this person's house? If the other person had lived there for a long time, you might not feel comfortable making changes to the physical space. As a result, it probably would never quite feel like home. When two teachers are assigned to teach a class together, it is common for them to use one of the teachers' classrooms (usually the general education teacher's); this often results in one teacher (usually the special education teacher) feeling like a guest in the other teacher's space. It is therefore far better to assign both teachers to a new, neutral classroom, and to provide them with the time necessary to set the room up together. The room should include a workstation for each teacher, and whenever the classroom is identified (such as on the nameplate outside the door or on a map of school), both teachers' names should be listed.

Equipment

Items such as study guides, texts on tape, and manipulatives can be very helpful in an inclusion environment. Because it is not always possible to anticipate what types of materials the inclusion teaching team will need, be sure to set aside funds for unexpected purchases.

Ensuring an Appropriate Class Composition

Effective inclusion classrooms are more heterogeneous than homogeneous. It is easy to lose sight of this fact and place students who do not qualify for special education but need services, or who may become eligible for special education at a later time, into inclusion classrooms anyway. Doing this creates a homogeneous, tracked classroom and nullifies the benefits expected from inclusion instruction in heterogeneous classrooms. It also makes teachers feel as though they are being "dumped on," resulting in lowered morale. Instead of this "reverse mainstreaming," it is often better to spread the students among several classes and consider the alternative scheduling options discussed earlier in this chapter.

You may be tempted to increase the number of total students assigned to inclusion classrooms—the logic being that with two teachers at the helm, class size can be increased while keeping the teacher-student ratio down. However, research suggests that effective inclusion classrooms should have fewer students than do typical general education classrooms (Scruggs & Mastropieri, 1996).

A final aspect to consider when ensuring an appropriate class composition is the severity of each student's learning difficulties. State laws often prescribe the number of students with disabilities that can be assigned to a given classroom, but do not consider the fact that all students with special needs do not require the same amount of teacher attention. In general, the more severe the disability, the more limited its presence should be in the classroom.

7

Launching Inclusion Teaching Teams

From small beginnings come great things.
—Dutch proverb

While chatting at their district's welcome back breakfast, two teachers are interrupted by their school's principal. He informs them that due to some last-minute scheduling changes, they are going to be collaboratively teaching a 4th grade classroom this year.

The teachers are in shock. Although both are believers in inclusion, they are concerned that they have never been trained in collaborative teaching before. Their undergraduate and graduate training addressed the research and legal aspects of the topic, but not the practicalities.

After reassuring the teachers that she's confident they will "make it work," the principal leaves them to speak with other staff members.

This is certainly not an ideal start to a collaborative teaching relationship. Instead of asking teachers to "make it work" and hoping for the best, you should provide a successful launch for your school's inclusion teaching teams. A well-planned initial staff development program will achieve this goal.

Staff Development

You will want your staff members to obtain expertise in collaborative teaching. High-quality professional development can help teachers achieve this. Over the years, teachers will progressively refine their collaborative teaching skills through the following steps:

1. Learning what constitutes collaborative teaching and what does not.
2. Using collaborative teaching strategies with students. You must convince teachers to risk short-term failure in order to obtain long-term success, and to overlearn new strategies until they become routine.
3. Assessing the efficacy of the strategies used and obtaining trustworthy feedback. Teachers should view "failures" as approximations that get successively closer to the ideal with practice.
4. Reflecting on lessons and how they can be improved by considering the discrepancy between the real and the ideal.
5. Implementing modified strategies.

Initial Training

Training team members together rather than separately can enhance performance. Initial training can take place over one seven-hour day prior to the start of the school year. Potential coteachers should sit together at tables, and you should provide them with a binder divided as shown in Figure 7.1, with copies of the attendant forms. Once the binders have been handed out, you will need an overhead projector, transparency masters of the forms in the binder, and a screen.

7.1 Contents of Initial Training Binder for Inclusion Teaching Teams

Section 1: Team Structure
- As a Teammate (2 copies)
- What Is an Inclusion Teaching Team? (1 copy)
- Potential Benefits of Inclusion Teaching Teams (1 copy)
- Goals and Parameters (1 copy)
- Our Vision (1 copy)
- Rules and Routines (1 copy)
- Roles and Responsibilities (1 copy)

Section 2: Student Information
1 IEP summary form per LD student

Section 3: Team Planning
- Inclusion Teaching Team Models (1 copy)
- Unit Plan (15 copies)
- Daily Plan (90 copies)

Section 4: Team Communication
Available Resources (1 copy)

Section 5: Team Reflection
- Developmental Stages of Inclusion Teaching Teams (1 copy)
- Inclusion Team Reflection Form (10 copies)
- Problem-Solving Worksheets (10 copies)

I have found the following agenda items work well for initial training sessions (they can be adjusted to meet local circumstances):

1. Getting Acquainted (15 minutes)
2. What Is an Inclusion Teaching Team? (5 minutes)
3. Potential Benefits of Inclusion Teaching Teams (10 minutes)
4. Goals and Parameters (15 minutes)
5. Rules and Routines (30 minutes)
6. Roles and Responsibilities (15 minutes)
Break (15 minutes)
7. IEP Summaries (120 minutes; depends on caseload)
Lunch (60 minutes)

8. Inclusion Teaching Team Models (15 minutes)

9. Inclusion Teaching Team Planning (60 minutes)

Break (15 minutes)

10. Available Resources and How to Access Them (15 minutes)

11. Coteaching as a Developmental Process (15 minutes)

12. Ongoing Assistance (15 minutes)

Agenda Item #1: Getting Acquainted

Purpose: It is critical for team members to become familiar with one another's professional instructional strengths, weaknesses, interests, and attitudes.

Duration: 15 minutes

Materials required: One overhead copy of a sample As a Teammate form (see Figure 7.2; a blank version of this form appears in Appendix 2, p. 145)

Steps:

1. Review the overhead transparency of the sample As a Teammate form with participants, who follow along in their binders.

2. Participants fill out each box on one of their copies of the form.

3. Participants share their responses with their partners. If there's sufficient time, they discuss their answers.

4. Participants return their completed worksheets to the appropriate section of their binders.

Agenda Item #2: What Is an Inclusion Teaching Team?

Purpose: This activity helps teachers reach a

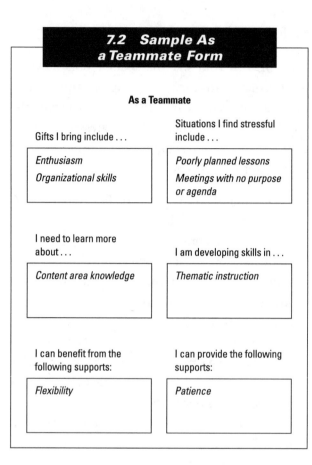

7.2   Sample As a Teammate Form

As a Teammate

Gifts I bring include . . .

Enthusiasm
Organizational skills

Situations I find stressful include . . .

Poorly planned lessons
Meetings with no purpose or agenda

I need to learn more about . . .

Content area knowledge

I am developing skills in . . .

Thematic instruction

I can benefit from the following supports:

Flexibility

I can provide the following supports:

Patience

shared understanding of what inclusion teaching teams are and are not, thus laying the foundation for the rest of the training activities.

Duration: 5 minutes

Materials required: An overhead copy of the What Is an Inclusion Teaching Team? form (Figure 7.3) from the training binder.

Steps:

1. Review the overhead transparency of the What Is an Inclusion Teaching Team? form with participants, who follow along in their binders.

2. Ask participants if they have any reactions to or questions about the definition. Discussion ensues as necessary.

7.3 What Is an Inclusion Teaching Team? Form

An inclusion teaching team is defined as follows:

A partnership in which a *general education* teacher and a *special education* teacher share *all of the teaching responsibilities* for *all of the students* assigned to a classroom

Agenda Item #3: Potential Benefits of Inclusion Teaching Teams

Purpose: Team members will be internally motivated if they view their work as meaningful and potentially beneficial.

Duration: 10 minutes

Materials required: One overhead copy of the Potential Benefits of Inclusion Teaching Teams form (Appendix 2, p. 146)

Steps:

1. Review the overhead transparency of the Potential Benefits of Inclusion Teaching Teams form with participants, who follow along in their binders.

2. After highlighting the potential benefits for teachers listed on the form, ask participants to record any additional benefits they can think of in the space provided on their copy of the form.

3. Turn to the potential benefits for students listed on the form. Participants record any additional benefits on their copy of the form.

Agenda Item #4: Goals and Parameters

Purpose: The objective of this activity is to communicate the team's goals and parameters to potential members. An example of a *goal* would be, "All students in collaboratively taught classes must demonstrate a 95 percent attendance rate"; an example of a *parameter* would be, "Team members must always use the common planning time provided for team business." Prior to the training session, complete the Goals and Parameters form and ask a trusted colleague to review it for clarity before including copies in the training binder.

Duration: 20 minutes

Materials required: Overhead copies of the Goals and Parameters form (Appendix 2, p. 147) and a filled-in version of the Our Vision form (see Figure 7.4; a blank version of this figure appears in Appendix 2, p. 148)

Steps:

1. Review the overhead transparency of the Goals and Parameters form with participants as they follow along in their binders. When done, ask if there are any questions.

2. Once participants understand the team's goals and parameters, review a completed version of the Our Vision form on the overhead projector.

3. Participants fill out the blank Our Vision forms in their training binders.

Agenda Item #5: Rules and Routines

Purpose: Teachers need to jointly develop the rules and routines that they will use in the classroom. If the teachers are not playing by the same rules, resentment and misunderstanding might ensue; in addition, if students perceive one teacher to be stricter than the other, they may exploit the situation.

Duration: 25 minutes

Materials required: One overhead copy of a sample Rules and Routines form (see Figure 7.5; a

7.4 Sample Our Vision Form

Keeping in mind the team's parameters and goals, fill out the boxes below.

As an inclusion teaching team, we hope to accomplish the following for *ourselves*:

Working together, we will develop our skills, share our knowledge, and learn from each other. We will share the joy and frustration of teaching a diverse group of students, all with their own unique talents and needs. Lastly, we will try to have some fun!

As an inclusion teaching team, we hope to accomplish the following for *our students*:

We will strive to meet the social, emotional, and academic needs of all of our students. We will also make sure that each of our students feels like a member both of our class and of the larger school community. No child in our class will dread coming to school.

blank version of this figure appears in Appendix 2, p. 149–150)

Steps:

1. Review the overhead transparency of the sample Rules and Routines form with participants, who follow along in their binders.

2. Participants discuss each item on the form with each other and fill out the blank copies in their binders.

Agenda Item #6: Roles and Responsibilities

Purpose: Coteachers must establish one another's roles and responsibilities after first carefully assessing one another's knowledge and skills. While the long-term goal is for team members to share most responsibilities, in the beginning it is usually better

to divide up the tasks, as this helps prevent anything from slipping through the cracks.

Duration: 15 minutes

Materials required: One overhead copy of a sample Roles and Responsibilities form (see Figure 7.6; a blank version of this form appears in Appendix 2, p. 151)

Steps:

1. Review the overhead transparency of the Roles and Responsibilities form with participants, who follow along in their binders.

2. Direct team members to discuss and select the appropriate box for each item on their copies of the form.

Agenda Item #7: IEP Summaries

Purpose: Teachers must be aware of the contents of their students' individualized education plans (IEPs). Because IEPs can be confusing to general education teachers, team members should complete a summary form for each student with an IEP and place it in their team teaching binders. This summary will provide the team with the information it will most frequently need. (Note: When completing these forms, teachers should take care to maintain student confidentiality.)

Duration: Approximately 15 minutes per summary form

Materials required: One overhead copy of a sample IEP Summary form (see Figure 7.7; a blank version of this form appears in Appendix 2, p. 152)

Steps:

1. Review the overhead transparency of the sample IEP Summary form with participants, who follow along in their binders.

7.5   Sample Rules and Routines Form

Class: Language Arts   **Teachers:** Jones & Smith

Period: 4

1. Seating Arrangement:

_____ Open seating

__X__ Assigned seating

2. When Entering Class, Students May . . .

_____ Visit with friends

__X__ Place personal belongings on desk and in lockers

__X__ Place class materials on desk

_____ Copy class work assignment from board

_____ Copy homework assignment from board

__X__ Other: Begin "Do Now" activity _____

3. At the End of the Period, Students May . . .

_____ Leave when the bell rings

__X__ Leave when dismissed by the teacher(s)

4. Procedures for Handing in Completed Work Will Be Discussed . . .

_____ Each time work is assigned

_____ At the beginning of each class

__X__ Only when the teacher requests that the work be turned in

5. Procedure for Requesting a Drink of Water:

Students must raise their hands and ask permission.

6. Procedure for Visiting the Restroom:

Students must raise their hands, ask permission, take the pass, and go one at a time.

7. Procedure for Visiting the Nurse:

Students must raise their hands, ask permission, and provide a written permission slip.

8. Procedure for Visiting the Principal's Office:

A teacher must direct the student(s) to the principal's office with a pass. The office must be called first.

9. Procedure for Visiting Lockers:

Students must raise their hands and ask permission, and may only go during independent work time.

10. Procedure for Sharpening Pencils and Requesting Supplies:

Students must raise their hands and ask permission, and may only go at the beginning of class or during independent work time.

11. Materials Needed for Class:

Textbook, pen, pencil, notebook, student planner

12. If Students are Missing Materials, They May . . .

Borrow from someone else up to three times before losing two points for each missing item.

13. Procedure for Late Arrivals:

Students may be tardy twice without a pass before being assigned detention.

14. Grading Policy:

90% or higher = *A*; 83%–89% = *B*; 75%–82% = *C*; 65%–74% = *D*; 64% or lower = *F.*

15. Procedure for Making Up Work:

For each day absent, students get one day to make up missed work.

16. Penalty for Late Work:

5 points will be deducted for every day that the work is late.

17. Testing Schedule:

A quiz is held every Friday. Tests are announced one week in advance.

18. Procedure for Asking Questions:

Students must raise their hands and wait to be called on by a teacher.

19. May Students Chew Gum or Have Snacks in Class?

No

20. Talking Is Allowed . . .

Only with teacher permission.

7.6 Sample Roles and Responsibilities Form

Ongoing Roles	General Ed. Teacher	Special Ed. Teacher	Both	Paraprofessional
Monitoring goals for each student with disabilities		X		
Developing new IEP objectives for students with disabilities		X		
Planning activities to achieve the goals			X	
Selecting and organizing instructional materials	X			
Teaching specific class content	X			
Teaching study skills and learning strategies		X		
Collecting data on student performance		X		
Establishing and implementing grading procedures			X	
Establishing and implementing a classroom management plan			X	
Maintaining home contact			X	
Participating in conferences			X	
Modifying curriculum, instruction, and materials as necessary		X		
Designing tests and assignments to meet individual needs		X		
Directing paraprofessionals, parent volunteers, or other support personnel	X			
Communicating with appropriate parties regarding the students with disabilities		X		
Daily Responsibilities	**General Ed. Teacher**	**Special Ed. Teacher**	**Both**	**Paraprofessional**
Attendance	X			
Field trip money	X			
Book orders	X			
Picture money	X			
Lunch cards				X
Walking/picking up students to/from lunch				X
Walking/picking up students to/from phys. ed., art, and music				X
Opening activities	X			
Grading papers			X	
Interim reports	X			
Stuffing folders				X
Maintaining cumulative folders		X		

2. Team members review each student's IEP together and transfer the relevant information to the student's summary form in the training binder. (For confidentiality reasons, teachers should use codes rather than student names on the summary forms.)

Agenda Item #8: Inclusion Teaching Team Models

Purpose: Due to either a lack of awareness or a discomfort with change, most inclusion teaching teams do not take advantage of the many inclusion models at their disposal. This activity helps teachers learn and apply six such models in class.

Duration: 15 minutes

Materials required: One overhead copy of the Inclusion Team Models form (Figure 7.8) from the training binder

Steps:

1. Review the overhead transparency of the Inclusion Teaching Team Models form with participants, who follow along in their binders.

2. Ask volunteers to share examples of how each model could be applied in the classroom. Participants should be encouraged to take note of suggestions relevant to their situations.

3. *Optional:* Show videotape of volunteer teaching teams using the models in the classroom.

Agenda Item #9: Inclusion Teaching Team Planning

Purpose: Inclusion teaching teams must view planning as a priority and must learn how to collaboratively plan instruction. Successful team members refuse to allow competing responsibilities to interfere with their planning; they remain focused on the task at hand and avoid discussion of unrelated topics.

7.7 Sample IEP Summary Form

Student: JEMA

IEP Goals (please state concisely and specify assessment method for subject areas)

Subject area: Language Arts
The student
- Will demonstrate the ability to write a three-paragraph essay. (*Assessment method:* writing rubric)
- Will demonstrate the ability to read a 5th grade core novel and satisfactorily complete a book project. (*Assessment method:* determined by teacher)
- Will demonstrate the ability to complete a 3- to 5-minute oral presentation with visual display. (*Assessment method:* district presentation rubric)

Subject area: Math
The student
- Will demonstrate the ability to apply knowledge of 5th grade fractions and decimals. (*Assessment method:* district quarterly math test)
- Will demonstrate the ability to apply knowledge of 5th grade geometry. (*Assessment method:* district quarterly math test)
- Will demonstrate the ability to use problem-solving skills. (*Assessment method:* math journal entries)

Subject area: Social and Emotional Learning
The student
- Will demonstrate the ability to work effectively in a cooperative learning group. (*Assessment method:* teacher observation form)
- Will demonstrate the ability to work independently during seatwork time. (*Assessment method:* teacher observation form)

Social and Academic Management Needs (please state concisely)
The student
- Does not perform well under time constraints.
- Will act silly to receive attention.
- Responds well when her misbehavior is ignored and appropriate behaviors are praised.

Accommodations (please state concisely)
The student
- Requires extended time on tests and quizzes.
- Should not be penalized for spelling errors (but correction is appropriate).
- Should be allowed to use a calculator for math assignments that are not assessing computation skills.

Special Needs and Additional Comments (please state concisely)
The student lost a grandparent close to the end of last year. She is very athletic and involved in many community sports activities.

7.8 Inclusion Teaching Team Models Form

Model 1

Teacher A presents the content.

Teacher B
- Paraphrases, clarifies, and elaborates.
- Injects questions anticipating student questions.
- Helps clarify concepts through the use of visuals and graphic organizers.
- Monitors and directs student attention to critical elements of the lesson.
- Notes students' background information at the beginning of the unit.
- Documents student progress and areas of difficulty throughout the unit.

Model 2

Teachers divide students into several groups according to their level of instructional need. After a period time, the teachers reassess groups and rotate the students so that the teachers can be aware of every student's academic level.

Teacher A teaches the whole class.

Teacher B
- Only visits the classroom two or three times a week.
- Oversees the guided practice of select students.
- Teaches select students strategic skills.
- Monitors the progress of select students.

Model 3

If the order of instruction does not matter, **Teacher A** and **Teacher B** can teach different content at two different stations in the classroom. A third station can be established for a volunteer or paraprofessional or as an independent station.

Model 4

For each lesson, teachers divide students into one large group and one smaller group of students who require additional support.

Teacher A teaches the large group.

Teacher B teaches the smaller group, focusing on adapted or enriched content and reteaching strategic skills when necessary.

Model 5

Teachers divide the class into two heterogeneous, equal-sized groups. Teacher A instructs one group and Teacher B instructs the other (both teach the same lesson). This model allows for a lower student-teacher ratio.

Model 6

During guided practice, both teachers monitor individual and small-group progress, hold student conferences, and provide individual and small-group instruction.

Duration: 60 minutes

Materials required: One overhead copy each of a sample Unit Plan form (Figure 7.9) and a sample Daily Plan form (Figure 7.10). (Blank versions of both forms are available in Appendix 2, pp. 153–154.) Participants will also need any materials necessary for planning instruction, such as curriculum guides or textbooks. Be sure to let teachers know about this ahead of time.

Steps:

1. Review the overhead transparency of the sample Unit Plan form with participants, who follow along in their binders.

2. Participants are allotted between 20 and 30 minutes to develop one instructional unit. As they do so, circulate, providing assistance as required.

3. Review the overhead transparency of the sample Daily Plan form with participants, who follow along in their binders.

4. Participants are allotted between 15 and 20 minutes to develop one or more daily plans. As they do so, circulate, providing assistance as required.

Agenda Item #10: Available Resources and How to Access Them

Purpose: Inclusion teaching teams will often require the help of outside resources for addressing student issues, but may not know how to access them or when it is appropriate to do so.

Duration: 15 minutes

Materials required: One overhead copy of the Available Resources form (Appendix 2, p. 155) from the training binder. Prior to the activity, you will have to determine who is available to provide teams with extra help, and how these people can

7.9 Sample Unit Plan Form

Unit Title: Physical Regions of the United States

Teachers: Mrs. Meidhof and Mr. Jackson

Dates: *From* 10/2 *Until* 11/6

Big Ideas (Concepts, Principles, and Issues):
• The United States is made up of nine physical regions.
• It is essential to protect national resources and to use them wisely.

Essential Learning Objectives (Knowledge, Skills, and Processes):
Students will be able to
• Interpret a temperature map.
• Name the nine physical regions of the United States.
• Articulate reasons why national resources are important.

Extended/Advanced Objectives:
Students will be able to
• Differentiate between renewable and nonrenewable resources.
• Compare and contrast different physical regions of the United States.

Objectives Adapted for Students with Disabilities:
Students will be able to
• Identify physical regions of the United States using a word bank.
• Identify the landforms and natural resources of one physical region.

Learning Strategies to Emphasize:
• Interpreting visual aids
• SQ3R

Concepts to Review:
• Latitude and longitude
• The compass rose

Activities:
1. Read pages 13–17 in the text and answer comprehension questions.
2. Complete a writing activity on the physical regions of the United States.
3. Watch a video on the physical regions and complete a cooperative learning activity based on it.
4. Learn about temperature maps in a whole-class lesson.
5. Read pages 18–21 in the text and answer comprehension questions .
6. Complete poster project.

Major Unit Project(s): Plan a family vacation from Boston to Yellowstone National Park

Major Unit Project(s) Adapted for Students with Disabilities: Plan a shorter family vacation

Supplementary Activities: Complete reports on up to four literature selections for extra credit

Assessments:
• Unit test
• Letter to a local conservation organization
• Family vacation plan

Assessments Adapted for Students with Disabilities:
• Modified unit test
• Recorded interview with member of a local conservation organization

Materials Required:
• Literature selections
• Video on the physical regions of the United States
• Poster board and markers

Materials Adapted for Students with Disabilities:
Audio versions of literature selections

---

be accessed. A brief explanation of each person's specialized knowledge is helpful as well.

Steps:

1. Review the overhead transparency of the Available Resources form with participants, who follow along in their binders.

2. Encourage participants to ask any questions they may have about the available services.

3. *Optional:* Service providers attend the training workshop and answer any questions. If this option is selected, additional time may need to be allocated for the workshop.

7.10 Sample Daily Plan Form

Date: 12/16/06

Subject: U.S. History

Class Period: 3

Unit: Growth and Conflict

Learning Objective: To demonstrate the ability to prepare an oral report

Purpose: To learn how to share information orally

Anticipatory Set: An imaginary report by Meriwether Lewis about his journey

Procedures:
1. Instruct students on the steps required to prepare an oral report.
2. Model the steps using clear examples.
3. Provide time for guided practice on a familiar topic.

Closure: Journal entry

Homework Assignment(s): Prepare a rough draft of an oral report

Learning Strategies That the Special Education Teacher Will Stress: The use of reference books

Methods That the Special Education Teacher Will Use to Support and Individualize Instruction:
1. Preteaching the steps for preparing an oral presentation
2. Helping students in a small group start on rough drafts in study hall

Methods That Coteachers Will Use to Share Instructional Responsibilities: The special ed. teacher will lead class during a lesson on the use of reference books.

Assessment: Peer and teacher feedback on rough drafts

Agenda Item #11: Coteaching as a Developmental Process

Purpose: Inclusion teaching teams usually proceed through fairly predictable stages of growth. Knowledge of these stages will diminish teacher and administrator frustration and may expedite movement toward true partnership.

Duration: 15 minutes

Materials required: One overhead copy of the Developmental Stages of Inclusion Teaching Teams (Figure 7.11) from the training binder

Steps:

1. Review the overhead transparency of the Developmental Stages of Inclusion Teaching Teams with participants, who follow along in their binders.

2. Participants discuss their reactions to the developmental stages.

Agenda Item #12: Ongoing Assistance

Purpose: Once the initial training is over, teams must have follow-up opportunities to reflect on their processes, discuss impediments to team effectiveness, and celebrate their successes. This activity provides a format for structuring ongoing assistance. I strongly recommend that you meet with teams at least once a month.

Duration: 15 minutes

Materials required: One overhead copy each of the Ongoing Assistance form and the Inclusion Teaching Team Reflection form (Appendix 2, pp. 156–157) from the training binder.

Steps:

1. Review and explain the overhead transparency of the Ongoing Assistance form with participants, who follow along in their binders. Indicate to teachers whether or not the meetings referred to on the form will be voluntary.

2. Review and explain the overhead transparency of the Inclusion Team Reflection form with participants, who follow along in their binders. Explain that this form will be used to examine team processes at each monthly meeting.

7.11   *Developmental Stages of Inclusion Teaching Teams*

	Typical Roles and Responsibilities	
Stages	*General Education Teacher*	*Special Education Teacher*
1. Beginning	• Writes the lesson plans • Instructs students • Informs the special education teacher of upcoming lessons	• Modifies classroom materials as needed • Monitors instruction of special ed. students by the general education teacher • Implements behavioral interventions • Grades and modifies tests • Interacts primarily with special ed. students • Develops separate lesson plans and maintains a separate grade book
2. Compromise	• Writes lesson plans and shares them with the special education teacher • Shares responsibility for some aspects of lessons with the special education teacher • Shares responsibility for daily guided practice activities for all students with the special education teacher	• Keeps a copy of the general education teacher's lesson plans • Reviews tests with the general education teacher to design modifications • Creates classroom visuals such as transparencies, written outlines, and study guides • Helps the general education teacher with classroom management • Shares responsibility for some aspects of lessons with the general education teacher • Shares responsibility for daily guided-practice activities for all students with the general education teacher • Develops and implements supplementary and supportive learning activities
3. Collaboration	*Both Teachers* • Jointly plan and deliver instruction • Monitor and assess all students in the class • Share ownership of classroom duties • Plan daily to ensure classroom coordination • Jointly develop lesson plans	

8 | Supporting Inclusion Teaching Teams

Habits can't be thrown out the upstairs window. They have to be coaxed down the stairs one step at a time.
—Mark Twain

Jack Greene is a principal. His goal is to sustain the momentum started by the initial training provided to his inclusion teaching teams. Having seen many initiatives start strongly only to fade, Jack knows it's easy for teachers to slip back into traditional instructional methods.

Monthly Meetings

To help ensure that teams continuously improve their skills, meet with them for 45-minute meetings once a month. The meetings should occur during work hours, so that teachers don't view them as "extra work." You may also wish to provide refreshments for a more welcoming environment. The meeting agenda should always follow this format:

1. Good News (10 minutes)
2. Reflection (10 minutes)
3. Group Problem Solving (25 minutes)

Agenda Item #1: Good News

Purpose: When reflecting on their work, teams risk focusing too much on what *doesn't* go well rather than what *does*. This can sap their motivation, so be sure to provide a structure for teams to focus on positive achievements.

Duration: 10 minutes

Materials required: None

Steps:

1. Prior to the meeting, teachers must think about their experiences on the team over the past month. (The principal should emphasize this fact at the first meeting.)

2. Each team member shares one success that he or she has had as a coteacher over the past month. Other team members are expected to listen to their colleagues carefully.

Agenda Item #2: Reflection

Purpose: Unfortunately, the press of task completion often keeps coteachers from conducting any meaningful reflection. Taking the time to reflect allows teachers to pinpoint areas of strength and weakness, which in turn helps them to set goals.

Duration: 10 minutes (if teachers complete the Inclusion Teaching Team Reflection form prior to the meeting; if not, more time may be needed)

Materials required: One copy each of the Inclusion Teaching Team Reflection form (see Appendix 2, p. 157)

Steps:

1. Ask team members to take out their independently completed Inclusion Teaching Team Reflection forms. (If necessary or desired, coteachers may complete the form at the meeting.)

2. Team members compare answers to determine areas of commonality and difference.

3. Team members spend a few minutes discussing and clarifying any discrepancies that exist.

4. Encourage team members to celebrate what they are doing well.

5. Ask team members to jointly identify one or two coteaching goals to accomplish before the next monthly meeting, based on the areas identified as needing improvement on the forms.

Agenda Item #3: Problem Solving

Purpose: Many inclusion teaching team members have not had much practice with group problem-solving strategies. Because barriers to success are inevitable for any group, it will often be necessary for you to help teams brainstorm strategies.

Duration: 25 minutes

Materials required: Markers and a piece of chart paper with three equal-size columns labeled "Issue," "Planned Action," and "Person(s) Responsible."

Steps:

1. Select one participant to take notes on the chart paper. (This responsibility should rotate among staff members from one meeting to another.)

2. Teaching teams take turns briefly describing the single most pressing problem that they currently face. These are listed in the "Issue" column on the chart paper.

3. Guide participants as they conduct a fast-paced brainstorm of possible actions to confront each problem. These are listed in the "Planned Action" column on the chart paper.

4. Participants come up with target completion dates for the planned actions and assign those responsible for completing them. This information is listed in the "Person(s) Responsible" column on the chart paper.

5. The information on the chart paper is copied onto notebook paper and photocopied, so that each participant has a record of the decisions made.

6. At the next meeting, the problem-solving session begins with quick update on the status of the planned actions.

Walk-Throughs

The implementation of inclusion teaching teams in schools is often a difficult, long-term task. Teachers will become frustrated, exhausted, and disenchanted at times; they may even wish to give up the journey altogether. You must inspire them through constant encouragement.

It is critical to observe teams in action and find examples of effective coteaching to reinforce. The primary vehicle for this is the walk-through—a brief visit to the classroom for the purpose of observing and providing honest, positive feedback to the coteachers. Regular, unannounced walk-throughs have the greatest effect on teacher performance. It is a good idea to block off time for walk-throughs on your calendar. Once in the classroom, focus on the positive; the only exception to this is if safety is at issue. The intent of the walk-through is not to conduct a formal teacher-performance evaluation, but to encourage persistence among teachers as they strive to create high-performing teams. The more specific the feedback, the greater the effect it will have on performance. Be sure to provide feedback either orally or in writing as soon as you note an example of effective coteaching.

Working with Additional Staff in the Classroom

Staff members other than coteachers, such as speech therapists and school psychologists, will often be working with students in the inclusion classroom, and may at times express their disagreement with actions that the coteachers take. You must make it clear that as long as the IEP and local policies are followed, classroom decisions are to be made solely by the inclusion teaching team. At the same time, you must also make it clear that coteachers should thoughtfully consider suggestions for improvement. In a professional school culture based upon norms of collegiality and mutual respect, this will not be difficult to achieve.

Often, one staff member will receive information related to the student and neglect to share it with others, assuming wrongly that they had received the information as well. For example, a parent writes a note to the speech therapist about issues with feeding at home, the speech therapist doesn't share the note with coteachers, the student has an incident during snack time—and the finger-pointing begins.

Meet with inclusion teaching teams and other staff members to establish protocols for sharing information in a timely fashion. The following questions could be used to guide this discussion:

• What criteria should be used to decide if the information is relevant?

• How soon after receiving the information should it be shared?

• How should the information be shared?

The outcome of this meeting should be a set of agreements on how information will flow among staff members. Once these agreements are understood by all, it becomes your role to monitor their implementation and evaluate their effectiveness.

9

Evaluating Inclusion Teaching Teams

Data are to goals what signposts are to travelers; data are not endpoints, but data are essential to reaching them.

—Mike Schmoker

Imagine if the results of a recently administered standardized assessment revealed that students in a collaboratively taught classroom did as well as or better than students in a classroom taught by a single teacher. By most accounts, this would be considered a successful situation in today's educational climate. But what if, in the process of achieving these results, the coteachers became so frustrated with each other and with the teaming process that they did not want to repeat it? In such a case, it would be hard to conclude that coteaching was truly successful.

Criteria for Effectiveness

Most of the tasks that coteachers are expected to perform do not have right or wrong answers; nor do they lend themselves to quantitative measures. There are three main criteria to consider when assessing team effectiveness:

1. **The actual outputs produced by the team.** These outputs traditionally include test scores, grades, and other measures of academic performance, but may also include behavioral referrals, school attendance rates, or any other student outcome that is clearly established and explained.

2. The health of the team. To be considered effective, the team's social processes must maintain or improve the coteachers' ability to work together on subsequent team tasks. A team's health is often best assessed through structured observation by the principal and self-reporting by members.

3. The effect of the collaborative teaching experience on individual team members. If team members primarily experience frustration and disillusionment with the group experience, then the costs of the process were too high. This criterion can be assessed through self-reporting by members.

Formative and Summative Evaluations

You will want to conduct both formative and summative evaluations when assessing inclusion teaching teams. The purpose of a *formative evaluation* is to help teams make changes in their design or delivery, thus increasing the probability of achieving desired outcomes. You must establish and implement an ongoing plan for collecting, analyzing, and sharing data that teams can then use to adjust their strategies. The purpose of *summative evaluation* is to assess whether intended results were achieved and whether material resources were used wisely in the process. There are three main components to successful evaluations: program evaluation questions, data collection and organization, and data analysis and action planning.

Program Evaluation Questions

Program evaluation questions communicate the intent of the evaluation and the information required to serve that intent. The following three questions, which are based on the three criteria for team effectiveness, should guide the evaluation:

1. Do the team's *productive outcomes* meet or exceed school and district performance standards?
2. Do the team's *social processes* maintain or enhance the coteachers' ability to work together on team tasks?
3. Does the *team experience* satisfy more than frustrate the personal needs of members?

Data Collection and Organization

Productive Outcomes

You can choose to collect and analyze academic, social, behavioral, or attitudinal outcomes, or a combination of the four, depending on which outcomes have the highest priority in your school or district. The charts that follow can help you to compare outcomes data from different types of classrooms: regular general education, regular special education, collaboratively taught general education, and collaboratively taught special education.

The chart in Figure 9.1 can be used to compare attendance and discipline data. The information should be collected for each quarter of the school year and used to make program adjustments as necessary. (If the data show that students with disabilities in collaboratively taught classrooms are being suspended more often than those in regular classrooms, for example, then that aspect of the program should be examined further.) The data from this chart can also be compiled and examined for trends over the school year, which can be valuable for the purposes of summative evaluation.

9.1 Student Attendance and Discipline Data by Classroom Type

Year: _____	Student Program Placement		Average Daily Attendance		Absent More Than _____ Days		Behavior Referrals		In-School Suspension		Out-of-School Suspension	
		Total No.	No.	%	No.	%	No.	%	No.	%	No.	%
1st Quarter	GE–Reg.											
	SE–Reg.											
	GE–Coll.											
	SE–Coll.											
2nd Quarter	GE–Reg.											
	SE–Reg.											
	GE–Coll.											
	SE–Coll.											
3rd Quarter	GE–Reg.											
	SE–Reg.											
	GE–Coll.											
	SE–Coll.											
4th Quarter	GE–Reg.											
	SE–Reg.											
	GE–Coll.											
	SE–Coll.											

GE–Reg. = General Education–Regular Class

SE–Reg. = Special Education–Regular Class (Resource/Self-Contained)

GE–Coll. = General Education–Collaboratively Taught Class

SE–Coll. = Special Education–Collaboratively Taught Class

The chart in Figure 9.2 is a summative evaluation tool that you can use for organizing data on grade-level student retention; it can be modified to suit whichever grade levels are most of interest. By analyzing the data, you can determine whether there is any significant difference in student retention from one type of classroom to another. Data should only be collected when the decision to retain a student has been made.

Use the chart in Figure 9.3 to note students' academic progress. Because it is not feasible to accurately compare the grades earned by students with disabilities in inclusion classrooms to those of their peers in more restrictive settings, this chart only focuses on the grades earned by students with disabilities. The chart is meant to be used once per marking period, making it a formative evaluation tool. (If data were compiled for the entire school year and then examined for trends or disparities, the chart would be a summative evaluation tool.)

Many schools conduct criterion-referenced assessments in grades 3–8. The chart in Figure 9.4 can be used to compare scores on such tests among different types of classrooms. Because these tests are administered once per year, this chart is a summative evaluation tool.

Another useful summative evaluation tool is the chart in Figure 9.5, which can be used to compare student scores on norm-referenced standardized tests. You should have four copies of the chart—one for each classroom type.

Although teachers don't often formally assess student attitudes, these may constitute an important outcome of collaborative teaching. The survey in Figure 9.6 can be used for this purpose, and the one in Figure 9.7 can be used to assess parent attitudes. If these surveys are conducted at the beginning, middle, and end of a school year, they will provide formative evaluation data; if they are conducted only at the end of the year, they will provide summative evaluation data.

Social Processes

Teachers involved in collaborative teams often report feelings of increased worth, rejuvenation, collegiality, and creativity (Friend & Cook, 2007). Yet they also report feeling frustrated with poorly defined roles and responsibilities, lack of clear expectations, and issues of implementation (Cook & Friend, 1998). This sense of frustration can be related to the gradual nature of the teaming process, which often begins with guarded, careful communication among coteachers, progresses to include greater compromise, and finally is characterized by open, honest interactions built upon feelings of mutual respect. In some cases, the coteachers "click" immediately; at other times they proceed slowly, struggling to effectively communicate and work together. It is not uncommon for the developmental process to take one year or more.

There are 10 major components to a successful coteaching relationship (see Figure 9.8), which are expressed differently at different developmental stages. Teams often show uneven development across components; for example, they may discuss classroom management issues openly and honestly, but instructional planning issues more guardedly.

(Main text continues on p. 78)

9.2 Student Retention Data by Classroom Type

	GE–Reg.		GE–Coll.		SE–Reg.		SE–Coll.	
	No.	%	No.	%	No.	%	No.	%
Whole School								
Kindergarten								
1st Grade								
2nd Grade								
3rd Grade								
4th Grade								
5th Grade								
6th Grade								
7th Grade								
8th Grade								
9th Grade								
10th Grade								
11th Grade								
12th Grade								

GE–Reg. = General Education–Regular Class

SE–Reg. = Special Education–Regular Class (Resource/Self-Contained)

GE–Coll. = General Education–Collaboratively Taught Class

SE–Coll. = Special Education–Collaboratively Taught Class

9.3 Student Progress Data by Classroom Type

Subject: _____

School Year: _____   Quarter (Circle One): 1st 2nd 3rd 4th

Grade Level		A		B		C		D		F	
		No.	%	No.	%	No.	%	No.	%	No.	%
K	GE–Reg.										
	GE–Coll.										
1st	GE–Reg.										
	GE–Coll.										
2nd	GE–Reg.										
	GE–Coll.										
3rd	GE–Reg.										
	GE–Coll.										
4th	GE–Reg.										
	GE–Coll.										
5th	GE–Reg.										
	GE–Coll.										
6th	GE–Reg.										
	GE–Coll.										
7th	GE–Reg.										
	GE–Coll.										
8th	GE–Reg.										
	GE–Coll.										
9th	GE–Reg.										
	GE–Coll.										
10th	GE–Reg.										
	GE–Coll.										
11th	GE–Reg.										
	GE–Coll.										
12th	GE–Reg.										
	GE–Coll.										

GE–Reg. = General Education–Regular Class
GE–Coll. = General Education–Collaboratively Taught Class

9.4 Criterion-Referenced Assessment Scores by Classroom Type

General Education–Collaboratively Taught Class

Grade Level		Partially Prof.		Proficient		Advanced Prof.	
		No.	%	No.	%	No.	%
3	Lit.						
	Math						
	Science						
4	Lit.						
	Math						
	Science						
5	Lit.						
	Math						
	Science						
6	Lit.						
	Math						
	Science						
7	Lit.						
	Math						
	Science						
8	Lit.						
	Math						
	Science						

Special Education–Collaboratively Taught Class

Grade Level		Partially Prof.		Proficient		Advanced Prof.	
		No.	%	No.	%	No.	%
3	Lit.						
	Math						
	Science						
4	Lit.						
	Math						
	Science						
5	Lit.						
	Math						
	Science						
6	Lit.						
	Math						
	Science						
7	Lit.						
	Math						
	Science						
8	Lit.						
	Math						
	Science						

General Education–Regular Class

Grade Level		Partially Prof.		Proficient		Advanced Prof.	
		No.	%	No.	%	No.	%
3	Lit.						
	Math						
	Science						
4	Lit.						
	Math						
	Science						
5	Lit.						
	Math						
	Science						
6	Lit.						
	Math						
	Science						
7	Lit.						
	Math						
	Science						
8	Lit.						
	Math						
	Science						

Special Education–Regular Class

Grade Level		Partially Prof.		Proficient		Advanced Prof.	
		No.	%	No.	%	No.	%
3	Lit.						
	Math						
	Science						
4	Lit.						
	Math						
	Science						
5	Lit.						
	Math						
	Science						
6	Lit.						
	Math						
	Science						
7	Lit.						
	Math						
	Science						
8	Lit.						
	Math						
	Science						

9.5 Norm-Referenced Standardized Test Scores

Percentile Range		1st–9th		10th–19th		20th–29th		30th–39th		40th–49th		50th–59th		60th–69th		70th–79th		80th–89th		90th–99th	
		No.	%	No.	%	No.	%	No.	%	No.	%	No.	%	No.	%	No.	%	No.	%	No.	%
K	R																				
	M																				
1	R																				
	M																				
2	R																				
	M																				
3	R																				
	M																				
4	R																				
	M																				
5	R																				
	M																				
6	R																				
	M																				
7	R																				
	M																				
8	R																				
	M																				
9	R																				
	M																				
10	R																				
	M																				
11	R																				
	M																				
12	R																				
	M																				

R = Reading   **M = Math**

9.6 Attitudinal Factors Survey for Students

Thank you for taking the time to complete this survey on your experience as a student in this classroom. Please answer **all** of the following statements by circling **one** of the five responses provided in the columns.

(A) Always	(M) Most of the time	(S) Some of the time	(R) Rarely	(N) Never

	A	M	S	R	N
1. I like working with the other students in this class.	A	M	S	R	N
2. I get along well with most of the students in this class.	A	M	S	R	N
3. I believe my classmates liked working with me.	A	M	S	R	N
4. I have friends in this class who I see at other times.	A	M	S	R	N
5. I enjoyed being in this class.	A	M	S	R	N
6. Both teachers listened to me and cared about my success.	A	M	S	R	N
7. I was able to participate in most class activities.	A	M	S	R	N
8. I successfully completed most class assignments.	A	M	S	R	N
9. I enjoyed having two teachers in this class.	A	M	S	R	N
10. I would like to have two teachers in my other classes.	A	M	S	R	N

11. What, if anything, was good about having two teachers in this class?

_____

_____

12. What, if anything, was bad about having two teachers in this class?

_____

_____

[End of survey]

Directions for Tabulating Survey Scores

1. Make one copy of the score tabulation sheet.

2. Using each returned form, tally the number of people who selected each response onto the tabulation sheet using the following formula:

   A = 5   M = 4   S = 3   R = 2   N =1

3. Count the total number of respondents for each question.

4. Multiply the number of A responses by the 5, M responses by 4, S responses by 3, and so on.

5. To obtain average scores, divide the sum for each question by the total number of respondents, rounding to the nearest 10th.

6. To obtain the overall score, add up the averages and divide the total by 10 (total number of questions):

   Less than 2.5 = Needs improvement

   2.6–3.4 = Marginal, may need to be improved

   3.5–4.4 = Average, no need for immediate improvement

   4.5–5.0 = An area of strength

9.6   Attitudinal Factors Survey for Students (continued)

Student Survey Score Tabulation Sheet

Question #	(A)–5	(M)–4	(S)–3	(R)–2	(N)–1	Avg.
1						
2						
3						
4						
5						
6						
7						
8						
9						
10						
	_____	/10 =	_____			
	Group		Group			
	Total		Rating			

9.7 Attitudinal Factors Survey for Parents

Thank you for taking the time to complete this survey. Your child was enrolled in a class that was taught by two teachers. As part of the evaluation of this program, we are seeking feedback on how this experience was for your child. Please answer *all* of the following statements by circling *one* of the five responses provided in the columns.

(5) Strongly Agree	(4) Agree	(3) Neutral	(2) Disagree		(1) Strongly Disagree		

	(5)	(4)	(3)	(2)	(1)
1. This class had a positive effect on my child's learning.	5	4	3	2	1
2. My child learned more academically in this class than in previous years.	5	4	3	2	1
3. This class had a positive social or emotional effect on my child.	5	4	3	2	1
4. This class had a more positive social and emotional effect on my child this year than in previous years.	5	4	3	2	1
5. My child expressed a positive attitude toward this class.	5	4	3	2	1
6. My child had a more positive attitude toward this class this year than in previous years.	5	4	3	2	1
7. This class helped my child to be more successful in other classes.	5	4	3	2	1
8. I communicated often with teachers in this class.	5	4	3	2	1
9. I communicated more often with teachers in this class this year than in previous years.	5	4	3	2	1
10. Given the choice, I would prefer to have my child in a collaboratively taught class again.	5	4	3	2	1

11. Additional comments:

_____

_____

[End of survey]

Directions for Tabulating Survey Scores

1. Make one copy of the score tabulation sheet.

2. Using each returned form, tally the number of people who selected each response onto the tabulation sheet.

3. Count the total number of respondents for each question.

4. Multiply the number of "5" responses by 5, "4" responses by 4, "3" responses by 3, and so on.

5. To obtain average scores, divide the sum for each question by the total number of respondents, rounding to the nearest 10th.

6. To obtain the overall score, add up the averages and divide the total by 10 (total number of questions):

   Less than 2.5 = Needs improvement

   2.6–3.4 = Marginal, may need to be improved

   3.5–4.4 = Average, no need for immediate improvement

   4.5–5.0 = An area of strength

9.7 Attitudinal Factors Survey for Parents (continued)

Parent Survey Score Tabulation Sheet

Question #	5	4	3	2	1	Avg.
1						
2						
3						
4						
5						
6						
7						
8						
9						
10						
	_____	/10 =	_____			
	Group		Group			
	Total		Rating			

The Coteaching Feedback form in Figure 9.8 can be used to provide feedback on the developmental stage of each major coteaching component; it can be used for self-evaluation, peer coaching, or formal teacher assessment. When teachers use the form to set appropriate goals for improvement, the form is a formative evaluation tool; when administrators use it to pinpoint areas of strength and weakness, it is a summative evaluation tool.

Team Experience

The Inclusion Teaching Team Rating Survey in Figure 9.9 can be used to assess how much the team experience satisfies each teacher's individual needs.

Data Analysis and Action Planning

Once you have collected and organized data, you must analyze the information and use it to make necessary changes, preferably in collaboration with the teaching teams. When coteachers are involved in data analysis and action planning, they have a greater sense of ownership for any resulting improvements. The processes described in this section assume that coteachers are involved; if they are not, adjustments will need to be made.

Data Analysis

When preparing to analyze data, consider three factors in particular: space, time, and materials. The room in which the analysis occurs should have enough blank wall space for posting information and enough floor space for moving around. The time necessary for data analysis depends on how much information there is to review and how many staff members are involved: a group of

between 15 and 20 staff members can accomplish the analysis in about an hour for the purposes of formative evaluation, and three hours for summative evaluation (which requires more data).

The materials required for data analysis include enlarged copies of the data displays, flip chart paper, and magic markers. Each data display will form a station along with three pieces of flip chart paper, one for each of the following discussion questions:

- What do the data on this display seem to tell us?
- What good news is here for us to celebrate?
- What needs for improvement might arise from these data?

For each data display posted, you will need one group (e.g., five teams for five charts). You can either assign group members at random or prepare the groups in advance. Random assignments encourage discussions among people who don't work together often, whereas advance assignments ensure that each group has the necessary characteristics to successfully complete the task.

Take the first five minutes of each data analysis session to explain or remind staff members of the purpose behind the activity: namely, to celebrate areas of strength, identify areas needing improvement, and develop action plans for enhancing the former and addressing the latter.

This is not an opportunity to evaluate individual teaching teams or staff members. If data analysis is to be successful, it must focus on the big picture, so that all teams can feel a sense of collective responsibility. None of the data should be able to be linked to any individual team.

Provide each group with a different color of magic marker. Once all of the groups are positioned at their stations, explain that they are to discuss the data shown and answer each of the questions on the flip chart using the marker provided. When you make a signal, the groups should move clockwise to the next station and repeat the process, writing their answers to the questions on the chart paper under those completed by the previous group.

Once all of the groups have rotated through all of the stations, each group must prioritize the areas identified as needing improvement in the first column of the Priority-Setting Matrix in Figure 9.10. (The process should take about 10 minutes.) Each staff member enters a rating in the columns marked "Effect," "Effort," and "Feasibility" for each area of concern listed, using a scale of 1 to 5, with 5 being the highest. Each participant then adds the three ratings columns together for each row and enters the sum in the column marked "Total of Individual Ratings." Based on these ratings, each staff member then selects his or her top three priorities, with the highest priority item receiving a score of 5, the second highest a score of 3, and the third highest a score of 1. Group members then discuss their conclusions and total the group results; the three highest priority areas thus identified will then serve as the top priorities for action planning.

Action Planning

Use the chart in Figure 9.11 to create an action plan for each item identified as needing improvement. Staff members must determine whether

professional development training or outside expertise is needed; if either is, it is your responsibility to secure such support. The action plans in this chart will serve as a focal point for all subsequent data analysis and action planning sessions.

Diagnosing Inclusion Teaching Team Problems

Mrs. Santos sits at her desk, thankful for the end of a long day. As she makes some last-minute notes to herself for tomorrow, Mrs. Hampson knocks on the door. From the look on Mrs. Hampson's face, it becomes obvious to Mrs. Santos that she is not going home anytime soon.

Mrs. Santos invites Mrs. Hampson into her office, and they proceed to engage in conversation. During the next hour, Mrs. Hampson expresses a wide variety of concerns about her coteaching relationship with Mrs. Johnson. Despite her best efforts to listen carefully, Mrs. Santos cannot find any pattern to the concerns. Mrs. Hampson's intense emotions only add to Mrs. Santos's difficulty understanding the real problem.

At the end of the conversation, Mrs. Hampson thanks Mrs. Santos for listening. Later, Mrs. Santos reflects upon their meeting. She realizes that although Mrs. Hampson probably found venting helpful, the two of them did not generate any long-term solutions to her concerns; indeed, Mrs. Santos is not even sure she knows what Mrs. Hampson's concerns *are*. She finds herself bemoaning the fact that, with the implementation of teaching teams in her school, she has added to her duties playing the role of therapist.

9.8 Coteaching Feedback Form

Teacher Name: _____ Tenure: _____ Nontenure _____

Teacher Name: _____ Tenure: _____ Nontenure _____

Grade/Subject Area: _____ School: _____

Observer: _____ Date: _____ Time: _____

NA = Not Applicable	B = Beginning	D = Developing	A = Advanced			
			NA	B	D	A
1. Interpersonal Communication			☐	☐	☐	☐
2. Physical Space			☐	☐	☐	☐
3. Student Arrangement			☐	☐	☐	☐
4. Curriculum Knowledge			☐	☐	☐	☐
5. Curriculum Modification			☐	☐	☐	☐
6. Instructional Planning			☐	☐	☐	☐
7. Instructional Presentation			☐	☐	☐	☐
8. Classroom Management			☐	☐	☐	☐
9. Student-Teacher Interactions			☐	☐	☐	☐
10. Student Assessment			☐	☐	☐	☐

Lesson Description:

_____

_____

_____

Strengths:

_____

_____

_____

Suggestions for Improvement:

_____

_____

_____

_____ _____   _____ _____

Date   Signature of Evaluator   Date   Signature of Teacher

                                                    _____ _____

                                                    Date   Signature of Teacher

Date of Conference: _____

9.8   Coteaching Feedback Form (continued)

Evaluation Rubric

Interpersonal Communication

Advanced	Through open and honest interpersonal communication, both teachers are positive role models for their students.
Developing	Both teachers demonstrate communication that is interactive but superficial; an increased use of appropriate humor is evident.
Beginning	Communication is guarded; each teacher struggles to correctly interpret his or her partner's verbal or nonverbal messages.

Physical Space

Advanced	Both teachers move freely about the classroom and share the appropriate resources and materials.
Developing	Teachers share some materials and resources. Although both teachers move freely throughout the room, only one commonly takes "center stage."
Beginning	The teachers' physical arrangements give an overall impression of separateness; both have their own materials and space.

Student Arrangement

Advanced	Special education students are normally seated throughout the classroom; adjustments are made based on instructional activities and student needs.
Developing	Special education students are dispersed throughout the classroom, yet the student arrangement does not change based on instructional activities or student needs.
Beginning	Regardless of the instructional activity, special education students are seated together.

Curriculum Knowledge

Advanced	Both teachers demonstrate understanding of the curriculum standards and the materials and best practices necessary to implement them.
Developing	With increased confidence in each other's knowledge of the curriculum, coteachers have an increased willingness to share the planning and teaching responsibilities.
Beginning	One teacher dominates the delivery of the curriculum and the instructional planning.

Curriculum Modification

Advanced	Both teachers differentiate between concepts that all students must learn and those that only some must learn, and use this understanding to modify content, activities, homework, and tests.
Developing	Due to a lack of appreciation for the fact that some students may require modifications beyond the IEPs, compromise is the norm between teachers.
Beginning	The instructional program is driven by textbooks and standards; modifications to the curriculum and accommodations for special education students are restricted to those in the IEPs.

9.8   Coteaching Feedback Form (continued)

Evaluation Rubric

Instructional Planning

Advanced   Both teachers share responsibility for all instructional planning and share ideas with one another.

Developing   Teachers are regularly responsible for planning certain aspects of instruction individually, and share ideas with one another infrequently.

Beginning   Due to a lack of shared planning, the special education teacher does not know how the lesson is organized or how the lesson will proceed. When small-group or individual instruction does occur, it is through a separate curriculum that is not parallel with the general education program.

Instructional Presentation

Advanced   Both teachers engage actively in the entire instructional presentation and select appropriate coteaching models to meet instructional goals.

Developing   Teachers share some of the instructional presentation, with each directing some classroom activities; both teachers use a limited number of coteaching models.

Beginning   When presenting instruction, one teacher is consistently in the role of leader and the other in the role of helper.

Classroom Management

Advanced   Both teachers share responsibility for the development and implementation of classroom rules and routines, and design individualized methods of behavior management when necessary.

Developing   Both teachers equally enforce classroom rules, but resist individualized methods of behavior management, preferring a group approach.

Beginning   One teacher assumes the role of "chief behavior manager" while the other delivers instruction.

Student-Teacher Interactions

Advanced   Students accept both teachers as equal partners in the learning process, addressing their questions and concerns to both.

Developing   Both teachers interact with all of the students, but more frequently with either the special or general education students.

Beginning   The special education teacher primarily interacts with special education students, and the general education teacher primarily interacts with the general education students.

Student Assessment

Advanced   Both teachers monitor and assess the learning of all students, using a variety of assessment strategies.

Developing   Teachers demonstrate an increased use of alternate assessments, but they are used the same way for all students regardless of need or ability.

Beginning   There are separate grading systems for special and general education students, and the only objective assessment tools are those that measure content knowledge.

Despite efforts to effectively design and manage teaching teams, there are bound to be potholes on the road to fluent implementation. You must be able to accurately diagnose the root causes of problems to generate a plan for addressing them. There are four main factors that influence the overall effectiveness of coteaching teams:

1. The availability and appropriateness of the resources that members use
2. The level of effort that members expend
3. The amount of knowledge and skill that members have
4. The appropriateness of the strategies that members select

These factors can only be assessed through focused discussions with team members and structured observations of their task performance. Once areas needing improvement have been identified, you can conduct a further analysis of the data.

➤ **Factor #1: The availability and appropriateness of the resources that members use.** Begin with this factor, because it is often the most straightforward to address. In doing so, ask the following questions:

• Do the resources the team members need exist somewhere in the school or district?
• Are the resources that exist in the school or district accessible to team members?
• Does the team have the planning time, physical space, and support personnel necessary to succeed?

➤ **Factor #2: The level of effort that members expend.** Although it is tempting to blame a lack of effort on the individual teachers, it is far more productive to examine aspects of the system as a whole. When assessing levels of effort, ask the following questions:

• Are the collective efforts of coteachers recognized in meaningful ways?
• Do coteachers have substantial autonomy for deciding how to complete their tasks?
• Do coteachers receive regular, trustworthy feedback about their performance?

➤ **Factor #3: The amount of knowledge and skill that members have.** Sometimes, teachers are assigned to coteach without having the necessary task-relevant expertise. Unless team members are reassigned, it may be too late to address a lack of knowledge or skill once the team is under way; still, it is important to assess teams in this regard for the benefit of future team formation. When assessing the amount of knowledge or skill among team members, ask the following questions:

• Are the teams appropriately tapping the expertise of their members?
• Do team members interact in ways that help them learn from one another?

➤ **Factor #4: The appropriateness of the strategies that members select.** When assessing this factor, the educational leader should ask the following questions:

• Do team members possess and use strategies for analyzing and generating solutions to problems?
• Do team members have the information required for selecting appropriate task-completion strategies?

9.9 Inclusion Teaching Team Rating Survey

Thank you for taking the time to complete this survey on your experience serving as a member of an inclusion teaching team. Please answer *all* of the following statements by circling *one* of the five responses provided in the columns. **Do not write your name on this survey.**

	(A) Always	(M) Most of the time	(S) Some of the time	(R) Rarely	(N) Never

	A	M	S	R	N
1. The task(s) to be achieved by our teaching team are clear.	A	M	S	R	N
2. The task(s) to be achieved by our teaching team are motivating.	A	M	S	R	N
3. The composition of our teaching team helps with the completion of our assigned task(s).	A	M	S	R	N
4. The composition of our class is reasonable considering the task(s) our team is expected to accomplish.	A	M	S	R	N
5. Our teaching team has access to the information we need for completing the task(s) assigned.	A	M	S	R	N
6. Our teaching team has access to the outside expertise required for completing the assigned task(s).	A	M	S	R	N
7. I feel rewarded for my efforts toward completing our team's assigned task(s).	A	M	S	R	N
8. Our teaching team has the necessary material resources for completing the assigned task(s).	A	M	S	R	N
9. It is clearly understood who is a member of this teaching team.	A	M	S	R	N
10. The norms and roles used by our teaching team are helpful for completing the assigned task(s).	A	M	S	R	N
11. As a teaching team, we have an opportunity to discuss with the school leadership any barriers that are impeding our performance.	A	M	S	R	N
12. As a teaching team, we receive assistance that helps us improve our group process.	A	M	S	R	N
13. As a teaching team, we stop to periodically reflect on and learn from our experiences.	A	M	S	R	N
14. I find the experience of serving on this teaching team personally satisfying.	A	M	S	R	N
15. The experience of being on this teaching team has increased my skills for working as a member of a team.	A	M	S	R	N

9.9 Inclusion Teaching Team Rating Survey (continued)

Inclusion Teaching Team Rating Survey Score Tabulation Sheet

Question #	(A)–4	(M)–3	(S)–2	(R)–1	(N)–0	Avg.
1						
2						
3						
4						
5						
6						
7						
8						
9						
10						
11						
12						
13						
14						
15						
	_____	/15 =	_____			
	Group		Group			
	Total		Rating			

9.10   Priority-Setting Matrix

Area of Concern	Effect	Effort	Feasibility	Total of Individual Ratings	Individual Ranking	Group Ranking

• Do team members regularly and systematically reflect on their task-completion strategies?

• Do team members seek and use feedback to improve their task-completion strategies?

In the introduction to this section, I described the creation of an inclusion teaching team program as a journey. What I did not say was how lonely this journey can be. When I undertook it, there were times I felt like the only one committed to the process. Early on, parents of general education students did not want their children placed in classes alongside peers with special needs, fearing that it would slow their children's academic progress. General education teachers also resisted making changes, often believing that the students with disabilities had not earned the right to be in their class. Although most special education teachers understood the need for change, they still yearned to be back in charge of their own classrooms. Building-level administrators were worn down by parent and teacher concerns, and in some cases used minor student issues as a pretext for returning to the old model. Ownership and accountability for the performance of *all* students was not easy for the principals to accept. Central office administrators resented the amount of professional development time and financial resources required to make the inclusion teaching model effective and often sought shortcuts.

More than once I was tempted to go back down the safe and easy road of pullout programs. What kept me from doing this? First, I consistently reminded myself that the goal must be to do what is best for the students. Because of past results and a strong philosophical base, I believed that the inclusion

9.11 Action Planning Chart				
Area in Need of Improvement	Action Steps	Individual(s) Responsible	Timeline	Evaluation

teaching team model was best for all students. This belief enabled me to retain my faith in eventual success. Second, early on I found a few key individuals within the district who understood and supported my ideals; in addition to being a great source of social support, they were the early innovators who made it possible to demonstrate that inclusion teaching teams could work. Third, I focused on recognizing early successes. Minor and continuous improvements bred commitment; attention and celebration maintained faith.

We gained momentum over time: hire by hire, tenure decision by tenure decision, the district achieved a critical mass of supportive teachers and support specialists. By sharing tangible results of positive achievement with parents and teachers, we converted many skeptics to believers. I even received calls from parents of general education students, requesting that their children be placed in "that classroom with the two teachers." General education teachers began volunteering to join the inclusion teaching teams. Over the course of five years, these teams became an integral part of the school district.

This section has provided you with the research and tools necessary to create and support inclusion teaching teams in your school. It cannot, however, provide the courage, conviction, and will to make these teams a reality. Ask yourself: Am I willing to do the work required to inspire commitment toward the common vision of inclusion teaching teams? Can I commit to communicating this vision enthusiastically and frequently? Am I willing to persist when others lose faith and question the wisdom of the model? The answer to all of these questions needs to be a resounding "Yes."

Shifting the emphasis from working alone to working together is a relatively simple idea. Implementing this idea is not. It may take years of experience before inclusion teaching teams are fully integrated in a district, but the persistence will be worth it to help our students and staff achieve the greatness they deserve.

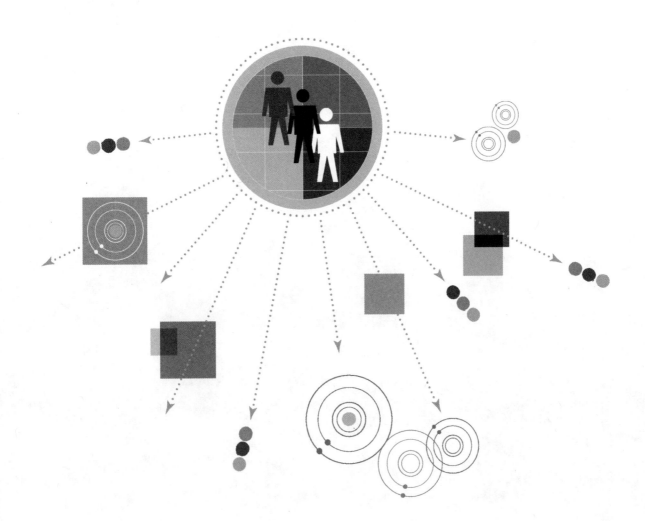

Section 3

Committees and Task Forces

Introduction

I recently conducted a staff development session at a middle school. During the break, I overheard two teachers discussing a new mandate from the central office. The mandate decreed that a committee of parents, administrators, and teachers should be established to "find ways to increase parental involvement in the middle school."

The teachers' conversation could best be summarized by a statement that one of them made. "This is the fourth time we have set up a committee to work on this issue," she said, in a tone of disgust with a hint of despair. "Nothing ever changes. Why will this committee be any different? I'm not wasting my time on that."

Through observation, research, personal experience, and discussion with colleagues, I have concluded that frustration with committees and task forces is common among educators. In my time as a school administrator, researcher, consultant, and staff developer, I asked many teachers what they thought of such groups. Sadly, very few ever responded favorably. This state of affairs has become so familiar to most educators that they are numb to the fact that committees and task forces aren't as good as they could and should be. The truth is, we can and should make committees and task forces better.

In this section, you'll find a sequential set of research-based strategies that you can use to transform your committees and task forces from barely tolerable to productive and meaningful. This transformation will significantly affect how you are perceived as an educational leader, and how your staff members interact as a professional learning community. You may even find that your committees and task forces can be defined positively, in a way that turns the epigraph on the next page on its head: as groups of the knowledge-able and skilled, appointed by educational leaders, to do the essential.

10

Understanding Committees and Task Forces

What is a committee? A group of the unwilling, picked from the unfit, to do the unnecessary.
—Richard Long Harkness

Mr. James thought he had approached the problem effectively. He was wrong.

It all started about three months after he had accepted a position as principal of a suburban middle school. As was customary in this district, Mr. James was required to meet with central office administrators at the end of September to review his school's performance over the previous year and establish new goals for the one to come.

Prior to the meeting, Mr. James reviewed the school data and found that the number of suspensions, detentions, and acts of vandalism at the school had increased significantly over the past year. He was therefore not surprised when Dr. Smith, the assistant superintendent of schools, declared at the meeting that this increase was unacceptable; in fact, said Dr. Smith, it was partly why Mr. James's predecessor had been let go after only one year.

By the end of the meeting, it was clear to Mr. James that if he were to succeed in his new position, he would have to address the school's discipline issues. During his drive back to school afterward,

Mr. James came up with the idea of forming a task force to do just that. Such a task force would help develop a plan of action while encouraging the staff to invest time in its implementation.

At the next day's weekly faculty meeting, Mr. James summarized his meeting with the administrators for his staff. After emphasizing the importance of reducing suspensions, detentions, and acts of vandalism, he shared his interest in forming a task force to address such problems. He asked that those who would like to serve on the task force submit their names to him by the end of the week.

On Friday, Mr. James was pleased to learn that 11 staff members had volunteered to serve on the task force. As the new principal, Mr. James wanted to ensure a school culture that truly treated teachers as professionals. To help achieve this, he decided to provide the task force members with a goal and let them proceed on their own. Over the weekend, he drafted a memo to the group members stating the goal, the deadline for achieving it, and the date on which the task force should first convene.

Time went by, without Mr. James receiving much feedback from the group. He would occasionally see a group member in the hall and ask him or her about progress, but that was about it. Though he had meant to attend a few of the meetings, he had gotten so busy with his other responsibilities that he just never got around to it. Because none of the task force members had come to see him with any problems, he reasoned that the group was doing well. What he didn't realize was just how bad things had gotten.

The task force members had all joined for different reasons. Six of them had been teaching for less than three years, and had joined so that they would receive favorable ratings on their end-of-year performance evaluations; two were considering positions as school administrators, and thought the task force work would look good on their resumes; and the other three viewed the task force as a way to "get tough" with disrespectful students.

In the beginning, the task force members also differed about what they were supposed to achieve. Several of the veteran teachers felt that their goal was to create a universal set of rules of conduct for all classrooms and determine the consequences for rule violations. A few of the other members thought the task was to create alternatives to detention and suspension, such as community service or in-school suspension programs. Two members thought they were supposed to explore social-skills programs for preventing problem behaviors. In the end, the group decided to follow the veteran members' lead and create a set of universal rules and consequences for the school.

After several meetings, the group had made minimal progress. Several of the members missed at least one of the meetings, and others either arrived late or left early. This behavior was partly due to frustration with three of the teachers, who tended to dominate the flow of conversation.

Recognizing that the task force's deadline was fast approaching, one of the teachers took it upon herself to take over and finish the task. The group was simply relieved that the process was over.

Mr. James looked forward to the staff meeting later in the afternoon, where the task force was to present its ideas to the entire faculty. He had intended to meet with the group earlier in the day to review its presentation, but had to cancel when an angry parent showed up at his office. Besides, he wanted the group members to know that he trusted them to do a good job.

At the meeting, after some routine announcements and reminders, Mr. James introduced the task force. As he listened to the group's presentation, the severity of his mistake dawned on him. Not only had the task force failed to address the task that he thought he had assigned, but it had developed a set of rules and consequences that clashed with his beliefs and values. From the body language of the teachers in the audience, he could tell that they weren't going to accept the task force's plan.

A Better Way

Mr. James's lack of knowledge in designing, managing, and leading a task force had caused him to make a significant professional mistake that damaged his credibility as a school leader. This was a loss that he would not easily overcome, and yet one that he could have avoided by making more thoughtful decisions and taking more appropriate actions. If he had designed and then managed the task force according to research-based principles of organizational behavior, Mr. James would have significantly increased the probability of a more productive outcome.

So why didn't Mr. James take these actions and make these decisions? Unfortunately, he didn't

know any better. Despite being an experienced educator with an advanced degree in educational administration, he had never learned the skills necessary to design, manage, and help committees and task forces succeed. As a result, he damaged his credibility with staff and didn't bring the school any closer to solving the original problem.

Defining Committees and Task Forces

Committees and task forces share many of the same attributes, but differ in duration and focus. Whereas *committees* focus on general tasks that require ongoing attention (e.g., language arts, school discipline), *task forces* address more specific concerns (e.g., lunchroom behavior, student scheduling) and are disbanded once they've achieved their goal. The guidelines in this book apply equally well to both types of groups.

Committees

Here are two examples of committees at schools with which I've worked:

▶ **Example 1: The District Council on Instructional Improvement.** This districtwide committee is composed of two teachers from each school in the district (elected by their peers to serve a two-year term), one school principal (elected by the superintendent for a two-year term), and the assistant superintendent. The committee meets once a month to generate recommendations for improving the district's instructional program. These recommendations are then shared with the school board for approval and adoption.

➤ **Example 2: The Intervention and Referral Services Committee.** The core members of this site-based committee are the school's principal, guidance counselor, and nurse, plus one general education teacher and one special education teacher. The group's purpose is to help teachers who are having trouble educating a student; members work with teachers to conduct problem-solving activities and coordinate school resources. This committee meets once a month.

Task Forces

The following are examples of task forces with which I've worked:

➤ **Example 1: Elementary Language Arts Textbook Selection Team.** Each elementary school principal in the district selected two teachers from different grade levels to serve on this task force. The team met with the assistant superintendent to review textbook series from different publishing companies using a district-created rubric. Using a consensus decision-making model, the team selected one series to recommend to the board for adoption. Upon completing this task, the group disbanded.

➤ **Example 2: High School Scheduling Team.** The superintendent gave one high school's principal the task of exploring alternative scheduling models and recommending an option for approval. To meet this mandate, the principal selected one staff member from each department to serve on a task force. Group members read research literature on a variety of scheduling models; after identifying some viable alternatives, they made site visits to schools that were already implementing them.

After recommending a new scheduling model to the school board, the task force never met again.

What the Research Tells Us

Committees and task forces are a fact of life in today's schools, and are reinforced by current trends in education: teachers are participating more in site-based management (Matthews, 1998), instructional approaches are more reliant on interdisciplinary collaboration (Pounder, 1998), and professional development models are emphasizing ongoing collegial interaction more than they did in the past (Evans-Stout, 1998). The formation, nurturance, and development of groups are at the very center of efforts to improve the quality of education (Johnson & Johnson, 1994a).

In a classic essay titled "Suppose We Took Groups Seriously," Leavitt (1975) raised the possibility that both people and organizations would be better served if groups, rather than individuals, were the basic building blocks in the design and management of organizations. Considering the research data, this appears to be a wise assessment.

An analysis of over 120 studies comparing the effect of group work versus individual work on individual productivity found that collaboration resulted in higher productivity levels than did competitive, individualistic work (Johnson & Johnson, 1994b). These results held true for verbal, mathematical, and procedural tasks. Johnson and Johnson also concluded that group work promotes more positive relationships and enhances psychological health, self-esteem, and social competencies more than competitive, individualistic work.

Qin, Johnson, and Johnson (1995) analyzed 63 studies examining the relative success of cooperative and competitive efforts on individual problem solving. They found that collaborative groups consistently outperformed competitive individuals on linguistic, nonlinguistic, well-defined, and poorly defined problems.

After analyzing 50 years' worth of studies on cooperative decision making, Johnson and Johnson (1989) found that groups are more effective at solving problems than individuals. Furthermore, even if solutions are not forthcoming, groups frequently serve as focal points for boosting morale and motivating workers to higher productivity levels.

Although small groups can yield the benefits cited above, they also have their drawbacks: they can waste the time and energy of group members, for example, or enforce norms of low rather than high productivity. (See Figure 10.1 for some other potential pitfalls.) Establishing small groups and using them successfully are two vastly different things.

Challenges Setting Up Groups in Schools

Educational leaders face several unique challenges when attempting to design, manage, and lead committees and task forces. For example, because teachers often work in isolation from one another, they may see committees as "add-on" activities for which they don't have time; indeed, Riehl (1998) concluded that teachers often view school committees and task forces as distractions from "real work."

10.1 Pros and Cons of Committees and Task Forces	
Possible Positive Results	**Possible Negative Results**
Increased individual and group productivity	Enforced norms of low productivity
More positive peer relationships	Poor decisions
Greater social support among group members	Conflicts between and within groups
Improved self-esteem and psychological health	Wasted time and energy
Enhanced social competencies	Lowered morale
Sharper problem-solving skills	
Heightened morale	

In addition, teachers and administrators often lack collaborative skills. They are frequently too quick to resolve differences by taking a vote or simply following their assigned "leader." Compared to workers in other fields, educators tend to be far less experienced (and thus less competent) working in small problem-solving groups, and are traditionally more willing to compromise the quality of work for the sake of maintaining harmonious relationships. Another problem lies in the unwillingness of teachers to trade individual for group accountability; educators do not easily take responsibility for the performance of their colleagues, nor do they want their colleagues to assume responsibility for them.

Unfortunately, the skills necessary to design, manage, and lead committees and task forces are seldom included in preparation programs for educators. Though such groups were never even mentioned in any of my formal coursework, I have had to implement them time and again throughout my career. In conversations with administrators across the country, I have never met anyone with formal training in this regard. More often than not, administrators say that they've learned how to lead groups through experience or by observing colleagues. Given that most administrators find their experiences with committees and task forces to be negative and ineffective, this is troublesome.

Attributes of Successful School Committees and Task Forces

The guidelines presented in the following chapters are intended for school- or district-based committees and task forces with the following five attributes:

1. The group is an intact social system, complete with boundaries, positive interdependence among members, and differentiated member roles.
2. Members of the group can be distinguished from nonmembers, even if members do not meet regularly in person or membership changes frequently.
3. Members depend on each other to attain some collective goal, and develop specialized roles within the group to pursue this goal.
4. The group produces an assessable outcome for which members have collective responsibility.
5. The group maintains meaningful relations with individuals or groups in the larger social system (that is, the school or district), and manages these relations collectively.

In this section, I explore the five-phase **D.E.C.I.D.E./ A.C.T./L.E.A.D./E.N.D.** model (see Figure 10.2) for creating successful work groups that fit the criteria outlined above.

10.2 The Phases of Effective Committee or Task Force Implementation

Phase 1: Analysis and Decision Making
- Determine the task to be accomplished.
- Establish the division of authority within the group.
- Consider the advantages, disadvantages, and feasibility of using a group to complete the task.

Phase 2: Planning and Preparation
- Identify group members.
- Design the task.
- Ensure access to necessary supports.
- Acquire material resources.

Phase 3: Start Up
- Clarify membership.
- Talk about desired outcomes.
- Lead in the development of norms.

Phase 4: Assistance
- Eliminate barriers.
- Assist with the work process.
- Dedicate time for reflection.

Phase 5: Evaluation and Closure
- Evaluate the group's effectiveness.
- Now, present results.
- Demonstrate appreciation for the group's efforts.

11

Analyzing and Decision Making for Committees and Task Forces

The first question in increasing productivity in knowledge work has to be, "What is the task?"

—Peter Drucker

A principal recently shared the following story with me:

> Many of the teachers in my school were concerned about the formatting and language on our student report card, so I put together a group of teachers to address the issue. I guess I wasn't clear with them about what they were supposed to focus on: I wanted them to change the layout and recommend revisions to some of the language, but they came back to me with a completely redesigned card—the new version included vastly different language, new grading criteria, and even a new set of learning objectives. The members of the group were really angry with me when I told them we couldn't use their example, but it would have been inconsistent with the district's expectations and standards to do so. If I had taken some time to explain what was expected before the group got started, things would have been a whole lot better for me in the long run.

This principal learned a hard but unnecessary lesson from her experience: unclear objectives can lead to lowered morale. If staff members put in the effort to come up with a product of which they're proud, only to find out that they have completed the wrong task, they are unlikely to volunteer for similar work in the future.

During the first phase of committee or task force implementation, your main objective is to analyze and decide upon the basic parameters of the group's performance. The letters *D, E,* and *C* in the D.E.C.I.D.E./A.C.T./L.E.A.D./E.N.D. model represent the following steps:

1. Determine the task to be accomplished.
2. Establish the division of authority within the group.
3. Consider the advantages, disadvantages, and feasibility of using a committee or task force to complete the task.

In the rest of this section, we will examine these three steps in detail.

Step 1: Determining the Task to Be Accomplished

Unfortunately, the task to be accomplished by a committee or task force is sometimes unclear. Of course, it is virtually impossible to design and support a work group if you do not know what the group's goal is, so the first step in designing a committee or task force is to establish one. Here are three principal criteria to consider when developing goals:

1. They should be specific. For example, a goal of "increasing parental involvement" is too general; a more specific goal would be "increasing the percentage of parents attending parent-teacher conferences." The more specific a goal is, the easier it is to evaluate whether it has been achieved.

2. They should be assessable by those who will be most affected by them. For example, I once worked on a task force of school administrators charged with creating a new online curriculum database for the district. Although we were quite satisfied with the finished product, the teachers who had to use it found it cumbersome and difficult. In the end, it was their assessment that mattered.

3. They should have specific deadlines.

The effectiveness of committees and task forces depends on the following three variables:

1. The level of effort that group members collectively put into achieving their goal
2. The amount of knowledge and skill that members bring to the group
3. The appropriateness of the strategies used to the task at hand

You should determine which of these variables are most critical to the assigned task. For example, a group tasked with assembling kindergarten registration packets for parents would rely more on effort than on the other two variables, whereas a group tasked with determining the readiness of young children for kindergarten would rely more on knowledge and skill, and a group tasked with clustering new kindergarten students for class assignments would rely more on the use of appropriate strategies.

Returning to Mr. James from the previous chapter, his first mistake was not taking the time to clearly establish and analyze the committee's goal. He should have taken the time to answer some critical questions, as shown in Figure 11.1. (A blank version of this figure appears in Appendix 3, p. 161.)

11.1 Sample Worksheet for Establishing and Analyzing Comittee or Task Force Work

Directions: Answer the questions below.

1. What is the work to be completed by the team? Be as specific as possible. This task force will analyze data from the previous school year on detentions, suspensions, and acts of school vandalism. Based upon an analysis of these data and a review of the related research literature, the group will formulate and present an action plan for decreasing the percentage of each of the three types of incidents by a minimum of 25 percent.

2. How will those who receive or review the team's work assess its quality? The task force will present its action plan to the entire faculty at a school meeting, where faculty will be divided into triads to discuss the plan's practicality and potential effectiveness. Each triad will assign a reporter to share its opinions; if necessary, the task force will use the feedback from the triads to revise its plan and present the revised version at a future meeting.

3. By when must the team have completed its work? The target date for the presentation to faculty is December 14th.

4. Will the level of effort that the team exerts significantly affect the effective completion of its work?

Yes   <u>No</u>

5. Will the amount of knowledge and skill of the team members significantly affect the effective completion of their work?

<u>Yes</u>   No

6. Will the appropriateness of the strategies that the team uses significantly affect the effective completion of its work?

<u>Yes</u>   No

7. Are any of the factors listed in questions 4–6 more critical to the team's work than the other factors? If so, what implications does this have for the design and management of the team? Yes. When designing this team, it will be critical to select members with knowledge about best practices in school discipline. Team members must also be skilled in using data to make decisions.

Step 2: Establishing the Division of Authority of a Committee or Task Force

Divisions of authority within committees and task forces will vary from district to district and school to school, but typically fall under one of the following three configurations: administrator-led, self-managing, and self-designing.

1. Administrator-Led. Members of these groups are only responsible for executing their assigned tasks; it is up to the administrator in charge to design the group, structure the context in which it functions, and monitor and manage the processes it uses. An example of this type of group would be an interview committee formed and led by a district superintendent to select a new elementary school principal. The members of such a committee would simply have to participate in the interview process as arranged by the superintendent. The success of administrator-led groups, then, depends more on the administrator than on decision making within the group.

2. Self-Managing. These are the most common types of committees and task forces in schools. In these cases, administrators are responsible only for the context and design of the group, and the group members are responsible for monitoring and managing their processes. Mr. James's group is an example (albeit a poor one) of a self-managing group. The success of self-managing groups depends upon the quality of the group design, the competence of group members, and the context provided by the administrator in charge.

3. Self-Designing. These types of groups are rare in education. In these cases, administrators have responsibility only for the context in which the group functions. An individualized education planning team would be an example of a self-designing group. The success of self-designing groups depends much less on the administration than on the group members themselves.

You must carefully consider how authority is allocated among group members and administrators. Sometimes, the type of hierarchy best suited to a group's work is at odds with school or district norms. (For example, a district in which most decisions are made by central office administrators would likely have difficulty implementing self-managing teams.) Such cases may require you to negotiate a redistribution of authority within the school or district.

To establish a tone of professionalism in his school, Mr. James created a committee designed to be self-managing. What he did not realize was that his district had a long-established tradition of top-down decision making. (On more than one occasion, his predecessor had told staff that groups were "for the weak" and "only served to hold back the shining stars.")

Mr. James's goal of enhanced professionalism is enviable; however, given the culture of his district, he should have formed an administrator-led group. Had Mr. James done this, he may have been able to address some critical questions as shown in Figure 11.2. (A blank version of this figure appears in Appendix 3, p. 162.)

11.2 Sample Worksheet for Allocating Authority for Committees and Task Forces

Directions: Read each statement below and select one response.

1. How much authority will the group need to have in order to complete its work well and on time?

High   <u>Moderate</u>   Low

2. Given the cultural and political realities of the school or district, can the necessary authority be granted to the group?

Yes   <u>No</u>   Not Sure

3. Will group members be willing to operate with the level of authority that *can* be provided?

<u>Yes</u>   No   Not Sure

4. Will group members be *able* to operate with the level of authority that can be provided?

<u>Yes</u>   No   Not Sure

5. Based on the answers to 1–4 above, the group will be:

<u>Administrator-Led</u>   Self-Managing   Self-Designing

6. What implications might the level of authority provided have for the administrator in charge? Although my long-term goal is to increase professionalism among staff, the school and district are not ready for this yet. I will need to look for possible ways to increase autonomy for this group so that future teams will be ready and able to assume leadership for self-management.

Step 3. Considering the Advantages, Disadvantages, and Feasibility of Committees and Task Forces

The chart in Figure 11.3 offers a list of the advantages and disadvantages of committees and task forces.

11.3 Advantages and Disadvantages of Committees and Task Forces

Advantages	Disadvantages
Allow for a broader perspective and greater input from staff	Can be time-consuming
Help members learn more about the decision-making process	Can encourage groupthink
Help staff make good decisions	Are more prone to taking chances than are individuals (the "risky shift" phenomenon)
Create a culture of collaboration and commitment	Can lead to group polarization
Increase morale	

Advantages of Committees and Task Forces

Committees and task forces offer the following advantages (Appelbaum & Batt, 1993; Harris & Sherblom, 2002; Katzenbach & Smith, 1993):

➤ **They allow for a broader perspective and greater input from staff.** The diversity of opinions in a group, along with the possibility of focusing the group's energy on a particular issue, can lead to excellent results. I have often been part of committees and task forces that generated more ideas than any individuals could on their own.

➤ **They help members learn more about the decision-making process.** Educational leaders often leave staff members confused or resistant to their ideas because the rationales behind them are not made clear. Teachers have frequently told me that they better understand the difficulty of making administrative decisions as a result of serving on committees or task forces.

➤ **They help staff make good decisions.** Committees and task forces allow for the testing of a large number of options. Increased creativity can occur, along with some excellent "piggybacking" by group members on ideas already formulated. On those occasions when I have been a member of a positive, productive task force, I have been awed by the quality of the decisions made.

➤ **They create a culture of collaboration and commitment.** Educators are more likely to trust and accept decisions that their own peers have made collaboratively than those handed down by administrators. I have often found that when teachers truly participate in decision making, they become strong advocates for the solutions they help craft and are more likely to follow through on them.

➤ **They increase morale.** Meeting with colleagues in groups can help lower interpersonal barriers, enhance school spirit, and help staff set common goals. Committees and task forces allow staff members to develop networks of people to call on at different times for other purposes. As a teacher, I often met valuable new contacts working on districtwide teams and remained in touch with them long after the group work was over.

Disadvantages

Among the disadvantages associated with committees and task forces are the following:

➤ **They can consume a lot of time.** Taking time away from other activities for group work is usually acceptable as long as the time is spent productively. Quick decisions rarely justify the use of groups unless "signing off" is desired. Because schools and districts value quick decision making, work groups can often rush to solutions. Unreasonable deadlines have caused more than one team I have served on to reach a poor decision.

➤ **They can encourage groupthink.** The combination of peer pressure and powerful group leaders can encourage group members to "go along to get along." Many of us can relate to the experience of not sharing potentially helpful ideas because of either the group's composition or its norms. A small, highly cohesive group can unconsciously undermine its mission in order to preserve a sense of cohesion (Aldage & Riggs-Fuller, 1993).

➤ **They are more prone to taking chances than are individuals.** This is known as the "risky shift" phenomenon: given the choice between certain loss and a risky alternative, the vast majority of groups will opt for the latter (Whyte, 1998). It is easier to take risks when responsibility for the outcome can be assigned to a group instead of an individual.

➤ **They can lead to group polarization.** More than 200 studies have found that people's propensities are reinforced when they are part of a like-minded group, leading to more extreme decision making (Gass & Seiter, 1999). For example, if a group leans toward risk, an individual who is already inclined toward taking risks will become even likelier to do so. (The same is true of groups and individuals that lean toward being more conservative.)

Feasibility

Committees and task forces are especially appropriate for staff members who have strong needs for both personal growth and significant social relationships, because collaboration allows them to satisfy both needs at once. However, it is unwise to form work groups if most of the potential members have strong social needs but low growth needs. In such cases, group members will likely use their experience to satisfy their social needs at the expense of the work to be done. Most educators can relate to the experience of being part of a group in which everyone got along and had a lot of fun, but nothing really substantial was accomplished. The same is true if prospective committee or task force members have low social needs but high growth needs. In such cases, it would be hard for groups to maintain the energy required to be effective because of the members' apathy toward working in social situations. In my experience, it hasn't been necessary for every single member of a group to have high growth and high social needs, because those who do not can often be influenced by the behaviors of other group members.

A group approach will sometimes clash with the overall climate and administrative style of your school or district. It would be difficult for committees and task forces to prosper in systems where individualism and competition are paramount, such as those with merit pay systems for teacher work. The same is true of schools and districts in which administrators vigorously enforce clearly defined procedures and authority is concentrated at the top.

Mr. James did not take the time to thoroughly assess the advantages, disadvantages, and feasibility of using committees or task forces in his school. The worksheet in Figure 11.4 shows what the results may have looked like if he had. (A blank version of this figure appears in Appendix 3, p. 163.)

11.4 Sample Worksheet for Establishing the Advantages, Disadvantages, and Feasibility of Committees and Task Forces

Directions: Answer the questions below.

1. What are the advantages of using a committee or task force to complete the work at hand?

• Because I am new to the school, staff members have a better understanding of the current situation than I do.

• Solutions will have greater credibility if staff members are involved in crafting them.

• The variety of skills and knowledge among potential group members will be helpful in examining an issue as complex as the reform of school discipline.

• Group work will help staff members to increase the sense of professionalism that I would like them to eventually embrace.

2. What are the disadvantages of using a committee or task force to complete the work at hand?

• As a new principal with many competing demands, I am not sure that I have the time necessary to manage a group.

• Staff members don't have much experience working collaboratively, and I'm not sure I have the skills necessary to serve as a facilitator.

• Because we need a solution soon, the decision-making process may be rushed and inadequate.

• Staff members are overwhelmed by competing demands and may not be able to devote enough time or attention to the group.

3. Given that it typically requires more administrative skill and time to manage a group than to manage individuals, do the advantages outlined above outweigh the disadvantages?

<u>Yes</u>   No

4. Given the culture of the school or district and the staff involved, will it be possible to design and support the committee or task force well?

<u>Yes</u>   No

12

Planning and Preparing for Committees and Task Forces

Teamwork alone never makes a team.
—Jon R. Katzenbach and Douglas Smith

A student in a graduate course I taught shared with me the following story:

I volunteered to serve on a task force to select a new grammar reference resource for our elementary literacy program. This group consisted of two teacher volunteers from each of the district's five elementary schools. When the day came for us to meet, we all seemed pretty enthusiastic about the task. Unfortunately, the day turned out to be a complete disaster.

First of all, the members of the group couldn't agree on how grammar should be taught: some thought we should use traditional worksheets, while others thought grammar should only be taught in the context of writing. Second, we had no criteria for evaluating the different resources; I thought we would have some type of rubric with which to rate each one, but this wasn't the case. Third, some of the resources we wanted to review didn't get shipped to us in time, so we had to evaluate them based solely on the description provided in the publisher's catalog.

I left that initial meeting frustrated by the total waste of my time. We never did select a reference resource. Most of the teachers are using materials they pick up from the local teachers' store.

Your primary objective in the planning and preparation phase is to make sure that the committee or task force is appropriately designed and has the support of the school or district. To achieve these objectives, you must analyze, select, and provide structures that will make it possible for the group to achieve high levels of performance. The *I, D, E,* and *A* in the **D.E.C.I.D.E./A.C.T./L.E.A.D./E.N.D.** model represent the following steps:

1. Identify group members with task-relevant expertise and collaborative skills.
2. Design a task that motivates and engages group members.
3. Ensure that the group has access to the necessary assistance and rewards.
4. Acquire the material resources needed to complete the task.

Step 1: Identifying Committee or Task Force Members with Task-Relevant Expertise and Collaborative Skills

The most efficient and obvious way to make sure a committee or task force has the knowledge and skills needed to complete its work is to select members with high levels of task-relevant expertise. You should assess the skill requirements of the task and then measure the capabilities of staff members for meeting those requirements.

Large work groups are common in schools. I was once on a 30-member task force formed to create a new high school schedule; the size of this group

allowed those in leadership positions to avoid difficult personnel choices and sensitive political issues. The downside of large groups is that they can lead to diminished efficiency and lower-quality solutions, as it can become nearly impossible to achieve consensus and coordinate activities. Research literature offers abundant evidence of the dysfunctions inherent in large groups, and supports the use of small groups (Hackman, 2002). When forming a committee or task force, make it no larger than absolutely necessary for accomplishing the task.

Consider the following scenario: a task force is meeting in the media center of a middle school. The group's assignment is to review and suggest changes to the school's policy on retaining students at grade level. All members of the task force are volunteers. During the meeting, a science teacher continually interrupts others while they are speaking, demeaning their suggestions and insisting that his solution is the only one that will work. Eventually, out of frustration, some of the group members begin to daydream about what else they could be doing. Others get agitated and start to argue with the science teacher. After about an hour, the group has made no progress, and everyone is completely frustrated.

Unfortunately, such a scenario is all too common in schools, because many teachers lack the skills necessary for effective collaboration. Even one or two such individuals can significantly impede a group's effectiveness. Given this fact, you should appoint group members with at least moderate levels of collaborative skill rather than rely on volunteers. This is especially important when groups are to be composed of individuals from different schools or departments that may have conflicting or competitive relationships with one another (such as in a committee formed to identify potential budget cuts).

Excessively homogeneous groups may have members who get along well with one another, but may lack the diversity of viewpoints necessary to complete their work—just as excessively heterogeneous groups may have a rich complement of talent, but may be unable to use that talent effectively because of conflicting values or perspectives. You should therefore strive to attain an appropriate balance between homogeneity and heterogeneity: groups should be diverse enough to ensure a variety of talents and perspectives, but similar enough that members can successfully understand and coordinate with one another. To achieve this, carefully analyze the four factors listed in Figure 12.1. (Of course, this requires you to have an accurate knowledge of staff members' skills.) Figure 12.2 illustrates what Mr. James's analysis may have looked like. (A blank version of this figure appears in Appendix 3, p. 164.)

12.2 Sample Worksheet for Ensuring Effective Committee or Task Force Composition

Directions: Answer the questions below.

1. How many staff members are required to successfully complete the task at hand?
Six staff members should suffice.

2. Which staff members have high levels of task-relevant expertise?
James H., Tom C., Melissa R., Holly S., Jodie J., Janine T., Ramona B., Jennifer M., Lynn S., Tom S., Jerry W.

3. Of the individuals listed above, which also have at least moderate levels of collaborative skill?
James H., Holly S., Jodie J., Jennifer M., Lynn S., Tom S., Jerry W.

4. Based upon your responses to the questions above, the committee or task force will be composed of the following members:
James H., Holly S., Jodie J., Tom S., Jerry W., Lynn S.

5. Does this group provide the appropriate balance between homogeneity and heterogeneity?
<u>Yes</u>   No

6. If not, is there anyone from the lists above who could be substituted to improve the diversity of the group's membership?

12.1 Four Main Criteria for Effective Committee or Task Force Composition

1. Members should have high levels of task-relevant expertise.
2. The group should have only as many members as are necessary to complete the task.
3. Members should have at least moderate levels of collaborative skill.
4. The group should be an appropriate balance of homogeneity and heterogeneity.

Step 2: Designing a Task That Motivates and Engages Group Members

Mr. Stevens and Ms. Woods, two teachers from the same school district but different schools, are watching their kids play in a soccer game on a Saturday afternoon. The focus of their conversation turns to their respective schools' district-mandated improvement task forces, the goal of which is to analyze student achievement data and develop action plans for improvement:

Mr. Stevens: Our team is progressing really well. We have analyzed our data, and are working as a group to develop our action plans.

Ms. Woods: Really? Our team is struggling. Our principal decided that we would each be assigned specific tasks based on what he perceived to be our strengths. No one really seems all that excited about finishing the work.

Mr. Stevens: I could see that. I think it's been great to work as a group on the whole project. It really made it possible for all of us to see the big picture of what we're trying to accomplish. Besides, I am not really all that good with analyzing data, so I've enjoyed working with colleagues who are more skilled in this area. I've learned quite a bit from them.

Ms. Woods: Did your principal give you detailed strategies for how to complete the work?

Mr. Stevens: No, she didn't. She met with us and explained what we had to accomplish, when we had to accomplish it by, and how the final action plans would be evaluated. Then she told us that it was our responsibility to decide on how to proceed.

Ms. Woods: You mean you were able to determine how to come up with the action plans? We were given specific strategies that we were required to follow. We started to wonder, "Who are we really completing this project for, anyway?"

Mr. Stevens: We were encouraged to come up with our own process, but our principal was insistent on what was to be accomplished and by when. She also met with us when we finished our data analysis; she assessed our work on that and suggested areas for improvement.

Ms. Woods: I think I would have rather have been on your team than on mine.

Like Mr. Stevens in the conversation above, committee and task force members can expect to be highly motivated, and therefore to work harder, when certain conditions are met. Consider the following five factors when attempting to create a motivating task for work groups:

1. Variety of skill and talent required by the task
2. Tangibility of outcomes
3. Effect of outcomes on those outside the group
4. Autonomy of the group
5. Feedback on outcomes when the work is completed

Group members' perceptions of their work's meaningfulness depend especially upon the first three of these characteristics:

1. Variety of skill and talent required by the task. When a task requires committee or task force members to stretch their abilities, members will find it meaningful (Hackman, 2002). An example of such a task would be one that required teachers to use a combination of problem-solving, communication, and decision-making skills in nonroutine ways. The more skills are involved, the more meaningful group members will consider the task to be. Even work that doesn't have a profound effect on the lives of others can still be meaningful to group members if completing it challenges their talents.

2. Tangibility of outcomes. Committee and task force members will care more about their task if it results in a *whole* product rather than just *part* of a product. For example, it is more meaningful to redesign an entire report card than to complete only the subtask of deciding on a list of optional teacher comments.

3. Effect of outcomes on those outside the group. Committee and task force members will find their work more meaningful if they understand that it will have a substantial effect on the well-being of others. Of course, most tasks completed by school or district teams will affect the lives of others, but it is easy to lose sight of this fact amid the day-to-day routine. Therefore, whenever possible, the educational leader should make explicit the connection between the task and its potential effect on others.

For group members to be motivated, the group must have at least one of the above three characteristics (Hackman, 1990).

4. Autonomy of the group. When the design of the task provides substantial autonomy to the committee or task force, members are likely to view the outcomes as depending largely on their efforts. The more autonomous a group is, the more group members tend to feel personal responsibility for successes and failures related to their work, so educational leaders should provide them with considerable latitude. Providing group members with autonomy does not mean simply handing over a task and sending them off with best wishes. Rather, you are faced with a balancing act: you must specify the ends to be achieved while allowing the group to choose work methods that they feel best match their skills and circumstances.

5. Feedback on outcomes when the work is completed. To be helpful, you should provide clear, direct feedback to group members about the effectiveness of their performance. Determine how to build feedback into the task. Members of committees and task forces must have methods for connecting the work they have completed with data about its efficacy: for example, if a committee selects a new textbook, a strategy should be in place for evaluating the impact of its selection.

Although the above five factors help to externally motivate group members, they do not necessarily ensure that members will be internally motivated, perform well, or experience satisfaction. To achieve these ends, members need to find the task exciting or otherwise rewarding.

The Importance of Clear Parameters

You should provide committee and task force members with clear parameters for their work. In particular, apprise them of the following:

- The task requirements
- Any constraints that may limit their options
- The material resources available to the group
- Who will receive, review, and implement the group's ideas, and what standards they will use to assess them

If you do not provide the group with this information, members may proceed in a way that seems reasonable to them at first but turns out to be completely inappropriate. For example, consider a committee that is tasked with recommending a new textbook for the district, but is not told that the new series must suit the district's budgetary constraints, available technology, and current curriculum standards. Such a group may proceed to recommend what it perceives to be the best possible resource for the students in the district, but at a cost that far exceeds the district budget and with content that does not address the district's curriculum standards. This type of dilemma can be avoided if you take the time to analyze and communicate the task requirements and constraints. Writing these conditions down before the group begins its work allows you to check the accuracy and clarity of the guidelines. Asking a "critical friend" to read over the guidelines and provide feedback is also a good idea.

Mr. James failed both to increase the motivating potential of the task and to make the parameters of the work clear for group members. Let us examine what it would have looked like if Mr. James had properly assessed the group's task using the worksheet in Figure 12.3. (A blank version of this figure appears in Appendix 3, p. 165.)

Step 3: Ensuring That the Group Has Access to the Necessary Assistance and Rewards

Just as supportive schools or districts provide committees and task forces with the information they need to get the most out of high-quality group designs, unsupportive schools or districts

12.3 Sample Worksheet for Designing a Task That Motivates and Engages Committee or Task Force Members

Directions: Answer the questions below.

(For the task to be motivating, the answer to at least one of the first three questions should be "Yes.")

1. Does the task require the use of a variety of skills and talents?
<u>Yes</u>   No

2. Does the task result in a whole, tangible piece of work?
<u>Yes</u>   No

3. Will the outcome of this task make a significant and meaningful difference to the lives of others in the school or district?
<u>Yes</u>   No

4. How can you redesign the task to meet the criteria in questions 1–3? The task already meets the required criteria.

(The task design must allow for both autonomy and feedback.)

5. Does the task design provide the committee or task force with substantial freedom, independence, and discretion in determining the procedures to be used?
Yes   <u>No</u>

6. Are appropriate feedback mechanisms built into the task so that the team will receive trustworthy feedback?
Yes   <u>No</u>

7. If necessary, how can you redesign the task so that it includes the necessary autonomy and feedback mechanisms? Task autonomy can be increased by developing subcommittees that are given specific assignments. These subgroups will then provide feedback to the whole group on their progress.

8. Write a clear, concise description of the task. Include the task requirements, any constraints that may limit group members' options, the material resources available to the group, and who will receive, review, and implement the group's ideas (and what standards they will use to assess them). The school behavior task force is charged with analyzing data from the past year on detentions, suspensions, and acts of vandalism at school. Based upon this analysis and a review of the related research literature, the task force will formulate and present an action plan for decreasing the frequency of the stated incidents by a minimum of 25 percent for each. Group members will be divided into triads to discuss the potential practicality and effectiveness of the action plan. Each triad will choose one reporter to share its opinion and suggestions. If necessary, the task force will take these suggestions and revise the action plan and present the revised plan at a future meeting.

can undermine even the most superbly designed groups. Therefore, committees and task forces must have both a high-quality design and a supportive school or district context.

Occasionally, the members of a group will have all the knowledge and skills necessary for excellent task performance. However, it is far more common that aspects of the task require additional talent or expertise. The staff development system of the school or district can play a significant role in helping the group to obtain such outside help. For this to happen, two conditions must be met: relevant educational resources must exist somewhere within the school or district (or be obtainable if not), and a method for delivering these resources to the group must be in place.

The particular type of assistance that the committee or task force requires will depend both on the task and on the group's needs. Sometimes, a one-time technical consultation will be sufficient; other times, a continuing relationship is required. For example, a group tasked with selecting a new math textbook may have content-related questions that require group members to meet with the district math supervisor, whereas a group attempting to design quarterly assessments of student progress may require ongoing consultation sessions with the district's assessment coordinator. You are responsible for providing groups with the full complement of knowledge and skill required for excellent task performance.

If a group does not have access to necessary data, it may develop a method for proceeding that appears reasonable to members but turns out to be grossly inappropriate when executed. For example, a group that is given the task of reducing school discipline referrals may mistakenly assume that the problem lies in inconsistent application of the school's rules, when the real issue is overcrowding caused by the school's routines. An examination of the school's discipline records would likely have revealed this pattern.

Schools have a tremendous amount of information at their disposal, yet they often do not use it to make decisions. Committees and task forces are no different than the larger school or district in this regard. Most of the work groups I have participated in did not use data to assist in their problem solving and decision making.

You should make sure that as much of the data required by the group as possible is readily available. Of course, this is not always practical: the information may not exist, may be costly to obtain, or may be politically sensitive. In such cases, the committee or task force needs to know that it will have to make its decision based on imperfect or incomplete data.

At the same time, care must be taken not to overwhelm the group with excess or irrelevant information. This risk can be minimized by initially providing the group with only basic resources, and instructing members on how to obtain more information as needed. In this case, the group is responsible for deciding what additional data are required.

Rewards

Consider the following scenario: a scheduling committee has just finished the difficult task of creating a master schedule that meets both staff and student needs. As a surprise, Mrs. Sampson invites all of the committee members to an ice cream party at the end of the school day. As the group members eat their sundaes and socialize, Mrs. Sampson praises them for doing a thorough job, and stresses how important their efforts are to the smooth functioning of the school system. The group members appreciate her gesture because they know how much she values their collaborative efforts.

Just as supportive reward systems can reinforce the motivational properties of committees and task forces, poorly structured systems can undermine motivation. Supportive reward systems have two features in common: they offer positive consequences for excellent task performance, and they focus on group behavior rather than individual behavior.

People tend to engage in behaviors that offer rewards, and teachers serving on committees or task forces are no different. The effectiveness of rewards depends on what group members value. Whatever the nature of the rewards, their effect on team effort will be enhanced if members understand that they are contingent on good performance.

If you provide rewards to individuals based upon your judgment as to who has contributed the most to the group, dissension and conflict can develop. Therefore, if it is not feasible to provide performance-contingent rewards to the group as a whole, it may be better to base rewards on the performance of the entire school or district. It is better not to use contingent rewards at all than to invite divisiveness.

Rewards in schools are usually not financial. In my experience, most teachers understand this. The ways in which you can acknowledge staff efforts are limited only by your own creativity.

Like most school administrators, Mr. James did not consider the context in which the task force would be operating. Had he done this, he would have realized that for the task force to be successful, he would need to make some changes to the information and rewards systems of the school. Figure 12.4 illustrates what it may have looked like had Mr. James done this. (A blank version of this figure appears in Appendix 3, p. 166.)

Step 4: Acquiring the Material Resources Needed to Complete the Task

Perhaps the saddest of all leadership mistakes in the design and management of committees and task forces is not providing members with the necessary resources. Without these, performance will surely suffer, even when the group is otherwise well designed. (For example, a talented, highly motivated task force formed to select a new assistant superintendent will not succeed if there are no qualified candidates to interview.)

Ask yourself: does the group have the tools necessary to complete the task? Does it have sufficient space for conducting meetings? Is the necessary clerical or technical support staff available to assist with the group's work?

12.4 Sample Worksheet for Ensuring That the Committee or Task Force Has Access to the Necessary Assistance and Rewards

Directions: Answer the questions below.

1. Can the reward system of the school or district provide the reinforcement the group will need to perform well?

Yes   No̲

2. If you answered no above, how can the reward system be modified? When the task is completed, I will hold a celebration with members of the group to recognize their success. I will also recognize their efforts at our staff meeting and in our parent newsletter.

3. Can the information system of the school or district provide the data the group will need to perform well?

Yes   No̲

4. If you answered no above, how can the group obtain the necessary data? I will provide the group with data on discipline issues at the school from the previous year, organized and compiled by secretarial staff.

5. Can the staff development system of the school or district provide the training the group will need to perform well?

Ye̲s̲   No

6. If you answered no above, how can the group obtain access to the necessary training?

7. What resources—space, raw materials, money, tools, or human assistance—will the group need to perform well? Because three of the group members have after-school commitments, substitutes will be needed when those members are unavailable. The group will need a space with a computer and a printer; the principal's conference room should be adequate.

8. Can the resources outlined above be provided to the group?

Ye̲s̲   No

13 | Launching Committees and Task Forces

It's easy to get the players. Getting them to play together, that's the hard part.

—Casey Stengel

Consider the following situation: the supervisor of the physical education department asks a group of teachers to revise the high school health curriculum so that it meets newly issued state standards. After explaining the task, he asks the members of the group whether they have any questions. No one does, so he assumes that his explanation must be clear.

Several weeks pass, and the supervisor decides to check in with the group. He is shocked to discover that they have simply taken the state standards for health and physical education and inserted them into the district curriculum. There is no integration between what worked in the past and the new standards. Furthermore, the sequence has not been organized so that important concepts build upon one another in a logical progression. He is disappointed, believing that the group took the easy way out. Meanwhile, the group members can't understand their supervisor's frustration; they believe they have done exactly what he asked them to do.

If this sounds at all familiar, then you have been part of a group whose leader did not take the necessary initial steps outlined in this chapter.

When group members first meet and confront their task, what can you do to increase the probability that they will work together effectively? At a minimum, establishing and building an effective committee or task force involves three specific steps—the C, T, and L in the **D.E.C.I.D.E./A.C.T./L.E.A.D./E.N.D.** model:

1. Clarify who the committee or task force members are.

2. Talk with committee or task force members to make sure they understand the goal.

3. Lead the committee or task force in developing positive behavioral norms.

Step 1: Clarifying Who the Committee or Task Force Members Are

If committee or task force members are to work interdependently to complete the assigned task, they must be certain who is and is not a group member. Group members are defined as *those individuals who share responsibility for completing the group task*. These individuals are accountable for the final product or decision.

Because group members are often also members of other, more permanent school teams, it can be unclear who belongs to what group. For example, members of grade-level, subject-area, or interdisciplinary teaching teams may receive input from others outside the team, resulting in confusion among team members as to how they should proceed. The group becomes frustrated because the "outsiders" do not fully understand the situation and are not going to be held accountable for the final outcome.

I once served on a task force with overly permeable boundaries. Our task was to establish redistricting guidelines—a politically difficult issue in the community. To ensure that all of the major points of view were represented, the district superintendent appointed representatives to the group from both schools and the community. At the first meeting, he specified that groups could include additional individuals from schools or the community if members believed that they could bring useful perspectives to the work.

Rather than bring additional members to actual group meetings, several group members would meet with the additional members independently. The feedback that the additional members provided was never appropriate, because it tended to focus on their own schools rather than the district as a whole. Furthermore, their suggestions lacked the insight that can only be obtained by participating in whole-group discussions. In the end, the group did not create new guidelines, because membership boundaries were unclear. Eventually, the superintendent grew frustrated enough that he hired an independent consulting firm to create the guidelines.

Step 2: Talking with Committee or Task Force Members to Make Sure They Understand the Goal

Redefining the task is a natural aspect of the group performance process. Acknowledging this fact and dealing with questions of task definition at the beginning of a group's life cycle will minimize confusion about the task requirements.

Consider a committee tasked with selecting a new textbook series. The series that the group chooses must be of high quality, and it must be chosen prior to the budget being submitted to the central office. In such a case, the educational leader should discuss with the group the potential conflict between having to choose the best textbook and having to choose it by a given deadline—in other words, quality versus speed. This discussion will result either in a resolution of the conflict or in the group's acceptance and management of it.

Mr. James did not help his group to accept and redefine the task to be completed. Because the committee members misunderstood what they were supposed to do, they wasted effort and created a product that clearly missed the goal. Mr. James should have taken the time to clearly identify the group's objective and deal with potential conflicts when the group first began its work, perhaps using the following activity.

Sample Task Definition Activity

Purpose: To achieve a common understanding about the task

Number of participants: 4 to 16

Duration: 20–40 minutes, depending upon group size

Materials required: Task Definition Form (see Appendix 3, p. 167), pens or pencils, chart paper, markers

Steps:

1. Read the group objective aloud and provide it to the group in writing.

2. Remove the written description and ask the group members to complete the following statement: "The task for this group is . . ."

3. Group members divide into pairs and share their responses with their partners. Within each pair, members write down the ideas they have in common.

4. Two pairs combine to make a group of four and repeat the process.

5. Groups continue to combine as necessary and repeat the process until the whole group is working together to identify common ideas.

6. Ask the whole group to share its ideas with you. Whole-group discussion follows.

7. If necessary, the group rewrites the task description so that all parties can agree on the group's objective and the task requirements.

Step 3: Leading the Committee or Task Force in Developing Positive Behavioral Norms

Each member of a committee or task force will bring to it a set of assumptions about appropriate behavior. These assumptions are rarely, if ever, discussed explicitly by the group. Group norms develop over time as members struggle to find a comfortable way to operate. This process is both natural and necessary, but the norms that evolve may be ineffective for the task: a group that avoids interpersonal conflict, for example, may preserve harmony at the expense of high-quality decision making.

Though it is the rule rather than the exception that norms will evolve over the lifespan of a group, you can get this process off to a good start by helping the group consider the behaviors that it will value early on. Use the activity below to help a group develop appropriate norms.

Group Behavioral Norms Activity

Purpose: To establish norms that will be conducive to group functioning

Number of participants: A minimum of four

Duration: 20–40 minutes

Materials required: Chart paper, markers

Steps:

1. Introduce the idea of staff meeting agreements as follows: "We have all been part of a team. In any team, there are certain rules or expectations for what we can or can't do."

2. Ask, "What were some of the rules or expectations on teams you have been a part of?"

3. Facilitate sharing of responses to the question above.

4. When all responses have been shared, continue: "What are some of the behaviors, both positive and negative, that you have experienced as a member of a team?"

5. Record the responses to the question above on a T-chart. Example:

Positive Behaviors
- Being on time
- Coming prepared
- Focusing on the task

Negative Behaviors
- Engaging in side conversations
- Dominating the discussion
- Doing work unrelated to the task

6. Initiate a group discussion about the messages that the behaviors listed in each column on the T-chart send to members of the team.

7. Lead the group in discussing the value of a set of basic agreements for group meetings.

8. After reviewing a sample of possible agreements, group members add other possible agreements to the list. The process continues until all members believe they have exhausted the possibilities.

Group Roles and Responsibilities

All groups function more effectively when members know each other's roles and responsibilities. Take sports teams, for example: in football, when the quarterback can anticipate the wide receiver's route, his throw is more effective; in baseball, the second baseman knows that the center fielder will back him up, so he takes the risk to catch the wide throw.

The following four roles are the most common in school committees and task forces:

1. The Facilitator. This group member expedites the meeting process and promotes the participation of all members. The facilitator may use strategies such as gatekeeping and consensus building to achieve active and equal participation among members. To solicit input, the facilitator may say something like, "Bob, I know you served on a committee like this last year. Do you have anything you would like to add?" To test consensus, the facilitator might say something like, "It seems that we have agreement on this issue. Is that true?"

2. The Recorder. This group member writes down meeting details, such as the names of those present and agenda items, and takes notes on relevant information and decisions. The recorder should produce written minutes of the meeting and make sure they are distributed to the members.

3. The Timekeeper. This group member watches the clock and warns fellow members when the designated time for each agenda item is close to over or has expired.

4. The Convener. This group member is in charge of securing the meeting place, providing for refreshments, and obtaining any required materials. The convener also helps plan the agenda for the next meeting.

The roles that a committee or task force decides upon will depend in part on the task to be completed. Group members should also decide whether the roles will be permanently assigned to certain individuals or will rotate among members. A meeting log can be used to note assigned roles, provide structure to meetings, and serve as a record that the educational leader can use to assess the group's progress. If Mr. James had completed this form, it may have looked like the example in Figure 13.1. (A blank version of this form appears in Appendix 3, p. 168.)

13.1 Sample Meeting Log

Date: 9/30/06

Members Present	Members Absent	Others Who Should Know About the Meeting
Jamie		
James		
Jerry		
Holly		
Lynn		
Jodie		
Tom		

Roles	This Meeting	Next Meeting
Facilitator	Lynn	Jerry
Recorder	Jodie	Lynn
Timekeeper	Tom	Jodie
Convener	Jamie	Tom

Agenda Items	Time Limit
1. Update on subgroup progress	10 minutes
2. Determination of next steps for each subgroup	10 minutes
3. Discussion of survey data	15 minutes
4. Closure	5 minutes

Action Items	Person Responsible	By When?
1. Updating nonmembers	Jodie	10/30/06
2.		
3.		
4.		

Agenda-Building for Next Meeting

Date: 10/12/06 **Time:** 3:15 P.M. **Location:** Principal's conference room

Expected Agenda Items

1. Update on subgroup progress
2. Focus-group planning
3. Discussion of parent and student survey results
4. Closure

14 Supporting Committees and Task Forces

Inventories can be managed; people must be led.
—H. Ross Perot

Two teachers who are members of a district task force are having a conversation after school:

Mrs. Jones: I'm not sure that I agree with our decision on the new class-size policy.

Mr. Smith: Didn't you do your master's thesis on class size and its relationship to academic achievement?

Mrs. Jones: Yes, I did. I think that's why I was asked to be a member of this task force.

Mr. Smith: So if you don't agree with the policy, why don't you tell the group why, and what you think might be a better solution?

Mrs. Jones: Are you kidding? I have been in this district for only four years. The other teachers on this task force have been here much longer than that. With all of their experience, I'm sure they must know better than I do what will work.

In this situation, the task force should strongly consider Mrs. Jones's knowledge of the research on class size; however, because she perceives experience in the district to be more important than such knowledge, she chooses not to voice her opinion. Unfortunately, such misperceptions are common in school and district work groups.

Once a committee or task force has been established, it will control its own future to a considerable extent. Yet you can still assist the group by taking three actions—the *E*, *A*, and *D* in the D.E.C.I.D.E./A.C.T./L.E.A.D./E.N.D. model:

1. Eliminate or minimize barriers to completion of the committee or task force's work.
2. Assist the committee or task force with its work as necessary.
3. Dedicate time for group reflection and learning.

Step 1: Eliminating or Minimizing Barriers to Completion of the Committee or Task Force's Work

Some of the features of a committee or task force's initial design are likely to be flawed. Most of the time, members accept these flaws as unfortunate realities of work in the school district. Although it may seem expeditious for the educational leader to unilaterally change the group's design, in the long term such action would undermine the group's responsibility for learning how to manage its affairs. Instead, you should provide scheduled, structured opportunities for group members to review and renegotiate the group's design, with a focus on aspects that are impeding the group's performance.

Mr. James did not provide his group with such opportunities. Like most educational leaders, he assumed that the members of the group would seek him out if they had a problem. Although it is unrealistic to expect such initiative from a newly formed group, or from members who lack the necessary skills, you should strive to instill a sense of resourcefulness as the group matures and demonstrates competence in its work.

Step 2: Assisting the Committee or Task Force with Its Work as Necessary

Interpersonal relationships in committees and task forces often leave much to be desired. Sometimes, members have such conflicts or become so competitive that they end up providing little support to one another; other times, they get so wrapped up in supporting each other emotionally that they risk neglecting their work. Thus, improving the interpersonal relationships of group members will help to improve the group's overall effectiveness. You should specifically help members to coordinate their activities, establish their commitment to the group, share knowledge and weigh the value of individual contributions, and assess the task and develop strategies for completing it.

Coordinating the Activities of Members

To minimize wasted effort, group members must coordinate their activities. Difficulties in doing so are inevitable. Because it is often the case that the larger the group is, the greater the difficulties are, you must be especially attentive to coordination issues in large groups. Often, the opinions and advice of people outside the group can be of help.

Establishing Members' Commitment to the Group

The level of effort that members expend depends on their level of commitment to the group. If members value their membership and find collaborative work rewarding, the overall level of effort will likely increase considerably. The educational leader can foster such commitment by helping members understand the importance of the task or by encouraging the development of a positive group identity. Some groups I have worked with have created team names, banners, cheers, logos, and even T-shirts as a means to establish a positive group identity.

Sharing Knowledge and Weighing the Value of Individual Contributions

It is important for groups to weigh the value of individual input effectively. Educators who are accustomed to working more or less on their own, or turning to a supervisor when they need help or information, tend to be neither skilled nor practiced at sharing task-relevant knowledge with each other. As in the example at the beginning of this chapter, groups often lend the input of certain members extra credence for reasons that have little or nothing to do with their task-relevant knowledge or expertise. These members may simply have more experience in education, important political connections, or a knack for presenting their views persuasively.

You should encourage group members to reflect on how they are using the contributions of individual members. Although more direct intervention may be necessary at times, it must be weighed against the risk of being seen as meddling in the affairs of the group. Over time, you should seek to train group members in how to share their individual, task-relevant skills with each other.

Use the activity below to assess the communication patterns within a group and facilitate reflective dialogue on the contributions of various group members.

Group Communication Pattern Activity
Purpose: To increase awareness among group members of current communication patterns

Number of participants: 4 to 12 people

Duration: 30–45 minutes

Materials required: Paper, pen or pencil

Steps:
1. Create a diagram of the group's seating arrangement, including the names of each person.

2. During the meeting, take note each time a person speaks and draw an arrow on the seating arrangement diagram to indicate to whom the person is speaking. (When the speaker is addressing the whole group, the arrow should point to the middle of the diagram.)

3. After a predetermined amount of time, present the diagram to the group and facilitate a discussion of it. Suggested discussion questions include the following:
   • "Was this a typical meeting?"
   • "What was the flow of communication like within the group?"
   • "What effect did the flow have on the group?"
   • "What changes would you suggest and why?"

Assessing the Task and Developing Strategies for Completing It

Because members of a committee or task force often have not had much practice developing and implementing innovative task-completion strategies, it is often necessary for you to help them do so. If the requirements and constraints of the assigned task have been made relatively clear, then a discussion based upon relevant questions will help the group formulate a process. Groups can use the worksheet shown in Figure 14.1 to structure this discussion. (A blank version of this figure appears in Appendix 3, p. 169.)

Based on my experience, the first few times a group conducts this discussion, members are likely to want to move rapidly toward generating solutions. Be sure to help group members remain disciplined in their thoughts and actions; it is important for the development of quality strategies that group members consider each of the six elements in Figure 14.1 carefully.

Following the discussion, the group is usually able to proceed on its own. It is important for the integrity of the process that you assist rather than direct the group. Your role should be to help the group "interpret" the task correctly and then develop or select appropriate strategies; to impose strategies is to risk compromising the group's autonomy.

Tuckman's Developmental Stages

You can help committee and task force members to deal with the inevitable developmental changes that they will encounter as the group matures. According to Tuckman (1965), most groups develop through the following four sequential stages (the typical timeline for each stage appears in parentheses):

1. **Forming (2–3 months).** During this phase, group members still don't know much about the other members or the group process; as a result, communication tends to be tentative and

14.1 Sample Worksheet for Developing a Performance Strategy

Situation (clearly define the task or problem): The school district's special education classification rate is disproportionately high for black students—three times higher than for any other subgroup in the school.

Options for Proceeding	Advantages	Disadvantages
1. Providing teachers with staff development in understanding U.S. black culture	May improve teachers' sensitivity to the learning needs of black students	• Costly • May not affect classroom practice
2. Improving the district's prereferral intervention process	• May lead to more timely assistance for black students • May benefit all district students	• Requires a time commitment from staff members • May require resources not included in the budget
3. Examining the special education assessment criteria to ensure that they are not biased against black students	• Easiest option to implement • May achieve results the most frequently	• May require the purchase of new assessments • May require the help of an outside consultant

Solution (may be a combination of options or a completely new one): We will immediately review district assessments and special education classification criteria to ensure that they are not biased against black students. If necessary, we will contact an outside consultant to help with this process. We will also analyze our prereferral intervention process and provide a long-range plan for its improvement.

We will know this plan is working when: The classification rate for black students is proportionate to that of other subgroups in the district.

characterized by a lot of agreement, as any conflict tends to be downplayed or ignored. Primary concerns at this stage include getting to know one another, becoming oriented to the group's goals, establishing operating procedures, and obtaining task-relevant information. Here is an example of a group at the forming stage:

It is the first meeting of the district-mandated school goals committee. The principal begins the meeting by stating the following: "As you know, our primary goal is to develop a plan for improving our students' performance on the state proficiency assessments. Are there any questions, comments, or concerns about this task?"

No one in the group responds. During a break, two group members have a conversation in the hallway. One teacher says to the other, "I have no idea what we are supposed to accomplish. Do you?"

"No," replies the other teacher. "Maybe it would help if he gave us some examples of what other schools have done to improve their students' scores. Why don't you ask him to do that?"

"*Me?*" says the first teacher. "Why don't *you* ask him?"

2. Storming (1–2 months). Once the "honeymoon period" of the forming stage is over, members begin to vie for control of the group. Members can become emotional or resistant at this stage, and the mood can turn hostile as disagreements are expressed. Even when the discussion remains focused on the task, individuals tend to take sides,

form coalitions, and align themselves with different factions; members must attempt to develop processes for resolving their differences.

This phase is the most complex, yet it is critical to success because it allows the group to air and clarify significant issues. Members must strive for consensus and try to prevent winners and losers. Here is an example of a group at the storming stage:

Members of a grade-level team are meeting in a classroom during their common preparation period. The grade-level coordinator tries to provide the group with information from her meeting with school administrators, but three of the teachers ignore her to discuss one of their daughters' wedding plans. Frustrated, the coordinator asks them to stop talking. The teachers ignore her request. Finally, the coordinator raises her voice.

"You would never let your students behave this way," she says. "Why do you think it is all right for you to do so?"

"I'm not going to be yelled at by you," responds one of the teachers. "Besides, you think you have all the answers and don't bother listening to our suggestions anyway."

After making this statement, the teacher leaves the meeting, followed by her two colleagues.

3. Norming (1–2 months). As the storming stage subsides, group members begin to sense that a positive development is occurring; though interactions remain tentative, members tend to express their opinions and cooperate more. The group becomes less polarized and more cohesive as disagreements turn toward possible solutions. Here is an example of a group at the norming stage:

The crisis planning and response team of a suburban middle school has been meeting monthly for half the school year. During the first few meetings, the group relied heavily on the principal to clarify the group's task. Once the expected outcomes were clear, the group had several heated discussions about how best to achieve them; at one point, things got so heated that it seemed as if the group would implode.

As cohesion and trust develop among the members, they eventually create a plan of action. The only thing left to do is decide on each member's role in explaining the plan to staff. Once this is completed, the group will be ready to share its work.

4. Performing (4–7 months). At this stage, group members share their viewpoints and information, seeking to achieve consensus on the final decisions and to follow through on them. Members feel a sense of relief as tension is replaced by group cohesion and problem solving predominates. Here is an example of a group at the performing stage:

Members of an interdisciplinary middle school teaching team are meeting during the common planning period. The purpose of this meeting is to plan end-of-the-year activities for the students assigned to the team.

The assigned team leader suggests that members outline all the things they need to do. When this

is completed, another team member says, "Okay, now who is going to do what?" A different team member responds that she'll talk to the principal and draft a letter to parents. The assigned team leader asks, "Who wants to pick up the supplies we need?" Two team members agree to divide responsibility for this task.

There are several ways in which group members can get stuck in a particular developmental stage, such as by cultivating positive feelings among one another at the expense of the task, spending an inordinate amount of time on conflicts, or remaining dependent on a group leader to tell them what to do. When groups get stuck in this way, their task performance suffers.

You must be sensitive to the developmental issues that groups will face as they move through their life cycles. Because committees and task forces develop over time, it is unrealistic to expect immediate results. Besides exercising patience, you may need to do the following:

• Provide members with an accurate, objective picture of how they are currently doing, with a focus on improving the team as opposed to individuals
• Supply the group with information on how groups normally develop
• Help the group to develop an action plan for using the information on group development to improve effectiveness
• Have the group commit to implementing the action plan, and help members remain focused in doing so

The following scenario shows a middle school committee that is stuck in the forming stage. As you read this scenario, note how the educational leader assists the group in its development.

The middle school health and safety committee consists of physical education teachers, the school nurse, guidance staff, and several members of the child study team. Members have been conducting a self-assessment of current practices for the past four months, with the goal of developing an action plan to improve coordination of services.

The chair of the committee is the director of guidance for the district. She approaches her supervisor, the assistant superintendent of schools, to share her concern that committee members are unwilling to express disagreement at meetings. Because members often share their feelings with the chair in private after each meeting, she knows that they have different points of view. The chair is frustrated not only because she believes the group would make more progress if it had open and honest dialogue, but also because the group members expect her to have to solve all their problems.

The assistant superintendent offers his assistance. He meets with the entire committee for half a school day and teaches them about how groups develop. He shares with them experiences he has had with other teams—what their problems were, and what each decided to do to fix them. He asks the committee members to select one or two issues they could focus on to improve their functioning. He works with them to develop plans designed to improve the group's processes in those areas. They decide to focus on respecting disagreements and

avoiding interpersonal attacks, and to put procedures in place for resolving conflicts as they arise. Under the direction of the director of guidance, the committee gets to work on implementing these ideas.

After two months, the assistant superintendent observes the group members at work and meets with them again. He shares with the team his observation that they have made significant improvements to their group process. The committee members agree with his assessment and decide to set new goals for further improving their collaborative skills. They develop and implement a plan to do just that—at which point the assistant superintendent knows his work with the group has been successful, and puts an end to his involvement.

Step 3. Dedicating Time for Group Reflection and Learning

Learning how to function together effectively is essential to the work of committees and task forces. Frequently, group members pay too much attention to the task and not enough to the process they are using. Achieving a balance between a focus on the task and a focus on the process is essential for group success. It is critical to the continuous improvement of group effectiveness for members to regularly reflect upon and learn from their experiences.

Because members are often too focused on completing their task to engage in meaningful reflection, it is often necessary to schedule reflection time. Although the amount of time necessary will vary, two ideal opportunities for reflective activities are at natural breakpoints in the task and when major task phases have been completed. At a minimum, reflection should occur both near the midpoint and at the end of a group's life cycle. Use the following activities to help group members reflect on their collaboration.

Reflection Activity for Midpoint of Committee or Task Force Work

Purpose: To help group members reflect on the processes they used to complete the assigned task

Number of participants: 6 or more

Duration: 5–15 minutes

Materials required: Chart paper, marker, pens or pencils, loose-leaf paper

Steps:

1. Post the following statements on a transparency or flip chart:
   - What I like about the way we are working
   - What I wish we would do more of
   - What I wish we would do less of

2. Randomly assign group members to base groups of three or more.

3. Each person finds a partner from another group.

4. Each new pair discusses the three questions.

5. When sufficient time has elapsed, all members return to share the content of their partner discussions with their base groups and prepare to report their findings.

6. Each base group provides a summary report to you. Discuss with members how the information from their discussions should influence the way they work together.

Reflection Activity for Conclusion of Committee or Task Force Work

Purpose: To help group members reflect on the processes they used to complete the assigned task

Number of participants: Any

Duration: 5–15 minutes

Materials required: Chart paper, marker, pens or pencils, loose-leaf paper

Steps:

1. Present group members with an appropriate prompt. (Example: "As a group, we did well on _____, but next time we could do better by _____.") Display this prompt in writing and also read it aloud.

2. Provide members with "think time" to complete a written response to the prompt.

3. Members break into pairs and share their responses.

4. Randomly select a few members to share their partner's responses.

5. As members share their partner's responses, write them down on a piece of chart paper.

6. The activity should conclude with a whole-group discussion about the responses.

15 | Evaluating Committees and Task Forces

What we call results are beginnings.
—Ralph Waldo Emerson

The work of a committee or task force is not over as soon as it produces the required output: the group's effectiveness needs to be assessed, its conclusions frequently need to be shared with others, and the efforts of group members need to be recognized. This brings us to the final three steps of the **D.E.C.I.D.E./A.C.T./L.E.A.D./E.N.D.** model:

1. Evaluate the group's effectiveness.
2. Now, present the results.
3. Demonstrate appreciation for the group's efforts.

Step 1: Evaluating the Group's Effectiveness

The effectiveness of a committee or task force should be gauged according to the following three criteria:

1. Did the group's results meet the standards of quantity, quality, and timeliness of those who are reviewing or using the results?
2. Did the group experience satisfy rather than frustrate the individual needs of group members?
3. Was the group's work enhanced by members' ability to work together in the future?

Your challenge is to develop ways to design and manage work groups that will help teachers meet or exceed these criteria. Consider Mr. James's committee at the start of this section: its output did not meet the standards of quality expected by the principal and the faculty, the individual needs of most members were frustrated, and the ability of members to collaborate effectively in the future was not enhanced. Clearly, Mr. James's group was not effective.

Although the presentation of results will often be enough to determine whether the group's output meets standards of quantity, quality, and timeliness, the other two criteria are often not assessed, despite being critical—after all, group members will often continue to interact as peers once the group is disbanded, and might even be asked to collaborate again in a different group.

To this end, it is important for the educational leader to assess group members' perceptions of serving on the committee or task force. The results of such an assessment can be used to improve the effectiveness of future groups, much as student evaluations are used to improve classroom teaching. Use the Committee or Task Force Rating Survey in Appendix 3 (p. 170) to evaluate group members' perceptions of their experience. The survey takes about five minutes to complete, and addresses key points discussed in this book. You can then compile the survey results using the Committee or Task Force Rating Survey Tabulation Form (also in Appendix 3, p. 171) and use them to determine the group's areas of strength and weakness.

Step 2: Now, Presenting the Results

Once a committee or task force has completed its work, it must present its recommendations to those who will be using or reviewing them. This is often done through a formal presentation, either by the entire group or by a subgroup. The presentation should include the following:

- An explanation or review of the group's work
- A summary of the procedures used by the group
- A summary of the range of options that the group considered
- A recommendation and a rationale for making the recommendation

The group's recommendation should include measurable objectives, critical steps for achieving each objective, time lines and responsibilities for each critical step, and methods for evaluating implementation. Group members can use the Group Presentation Form in Appendix 3 (p. 173) to organize this information. Visual aids such as charts, graphs, diagrams, and overhead transparencies are often helpful. Here are some tips for creating effective visual aids:

- Visual aids should be large enough for everyone in the audience to see with relative ease.
- Visual aids should be simple and should introduce only the essential elements of the concepts being discussed.
- The audience should be able to read what is written on visual aids. Presenters should carefully consider the font, size, and color of the text. Consistency is critical.

• Simple, brief, carefully proofread handouts can enhance a group presentation. If a long handout is necessary, then the group should also provide an executive summary.

It is especially irksome when a group allots time and effort to reach a high-quality solution, only to have it judged unfairly because of the way it is presented. Whenever possible, have committees or task forces make their presentations to you first, in private. This will enable you to help members fine-tune their presentations and ultimately ensure that they receive thoughtful consideration. During the private presentation, be sure to stress the following points:

• Presenters should avoid reading to the audience. Some notes or an outline are appropriate, but a prepared script is not.
• Presenters should avoid jargon specific to the group's work unless it is also familiar to the audience.
• Presenters should project enthusiasm for their group's output. A lack of enthusiasm among the presenters may negatively influence audience perceptions.
• All presenters should know what everyone else is going to say.
• Presenters should expect questions from the audience following their presentation.

If necessary, remind members to check out the location of the meeting in advance, to make sure that it is set up appropriately and that the audiovisual equipment is working.

Step 3. Demonstrating Appreciation for the Group's Efforts

Committee and task force members are more likely to build a long-term commitment to group work when they feel successful, appreciated, and respected. In celebrating the group's accomplishments, avoid comparisons among team members and monitor your language: by avoiding words like "winner," "best," or "first," you will diminish resentment among group members.

Don't just set up the celebration—join in! How you choose to spend your time is symbolic of what you value. When the educational leader joins in the celebration, he or she focuses the attention of group members on the importance of teamwork and shows commitment to using groups to address school issues. Here are some suggestions for celebrating a group's accomplishments:

• A thank-you letter published in the school newsletter
• Certificates of appreciation presented at a school faculty or board of education meeting
• A luncheon, breakfast, or after-school ice cream party with members of the group
• An acknowledgment published on the school or district Web site

This section presents a framework you can follow when designing, managing, and leading school committees and task forces. In each phase of the framework, you must take action to encourage effective group work.

Schools are not simply buildings, curriculums, and equipment; they are relationships among people. How educators interact with one another will ultimately determine how effective a school becomes. Although all educators are heroes deserving of gratitude and respect, the challenges facing schools have become far too complex for individuals to solve on their own. Committees and task forces are necessary to meet these challenges. It is the responsibility of 21st-century educational leaders to harness and nurture the power of these groups. To do so, leaders will need to employ considerable managerial skills and abundant energy.

Though the framework presented in this section may seem unfamiliar and possibly even awkward to some, the same can be said of a new budgeting process (to take one example). Any new endeavor can seem difficult at first. As staff members gain experience and skills working with groups, the steps laid out here will become second nature and will reap dividends for educational leaders, staff members, and ultimately, students.

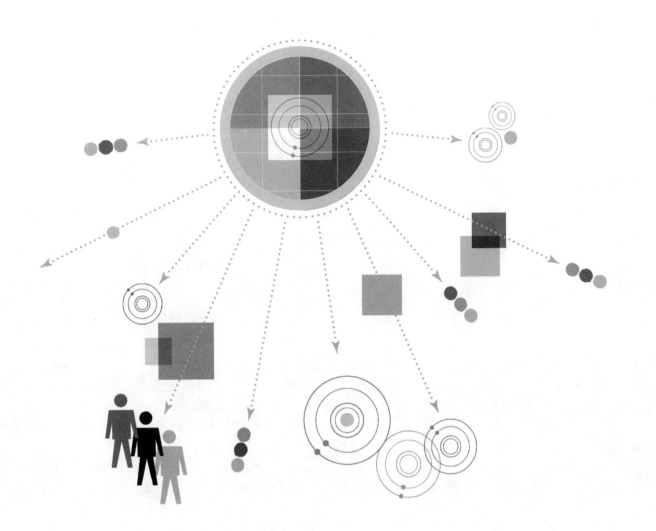

Appendix 1

Study Group Selection Survey

Name: _____

Directions: Read all of the choices below. Check the box next to the topics you would like to analyze further in teacher study groups. You must select a minimum of three topics, but feel free to choose more.

Alternative Assessment/Evaluation ☐

Classroom Management ☐

Cooperative Learning ☐

Curriculum Integration ☐

Differentiated Instruction ☐

Diversity/Equity Issues ☐

Inclusion/Special Education ☐

Multiple Intelligences/Learning Styles ☐

Promoting Positive Parent Involvement ☐

Technology ☐

Other (Please describe) _____

_____

_____

_____

_____

Study Group Organization Chart

Alternative Assessment	Classroom Management	Cooperative Learning	Curriculum Integration
Differentiated Instruction	**Diversity/Equity Issues**	**Inclusion/Special Ed.**	**M.I./Learning Styles**
Parental Involvement	**Technology**	**Other**	**Other**

Study Group Log

Reading(s): _____

Date: _____

Members Present

_____

_____

_____

_____

Members Absent

_____

_____

_____

_____

Roles	This Meeting	Next Meeting
Facilitator	_____	_____
Recorder	_____	_____
Reporter	_____	_____
Materials Manager	_____	_____

Key points of discussion:

1. _____

_____

2. _____

_____

3. _____

_____

4. _____

_____

Steps to take based on readings:

1. _____

_____

2. _____

_____

Date of next meeting: _____

Reading assignment: _____

Study Group Reading Schedule Form

Date

Reading(s)

Faculty Meeting Rating Survey

Thank you for taking the time to complete this survey on faculty meetings. Please answer *all* of the following statements by circling *one* of the five responses provided in the columns.

A = Always   M = Most of the time   S = Sometimes   R = Rarely   N = Never

1. There is a clear purpose to meetings.	A	M	S	R	N
2. An agenda is distributed prior to meetings.	A	M	S	R	N
3. Staff members have the opportunity to provide input on faculty meeting topics.	A	M	S	R	N
4. The seating arrangement at meetings is appropriate for the activities being conducted.	A	M	S	R	N
5. The physical environment of the room in which meetings are held is comfortable.	A	M	S	R	N
6. Refreshments are provided at meetings.	A	M	S	R	N
7. The order in which agenda topics are presented helps achieve the desired outcomes of meetings.	A	M	S	R	N
8. Faculty meetings start on time.	A	M	S	R	N
9. Faculty meetings end on time.	A	M	S	R	N
10. The amount of time devoted to meeting topics is appropriate.	A	M	S	R	N
11. The emotional climate at meetings encourages the sharing of opinions.	A	M	S	R	N
12. Discussions are structured to encourage equal participation.	A	M	S	R	N
13. Discussion methods vary depending on the desired outcomes.	A	M	S	R	N
14. Discussions remain focused on agenda topics.	A	M	S	R	N
15. Attendees actively listen to each other's ideas and opinions.	A	M	S	R	N
16. Conflicts and disagreements are handled constructively.	A	M	S	R	N
17. At the end of meetings, attendees are clear on assignments, responsibilities, and next steps.	A	M	S	R	N
18. Meeting minutes are distributed to staff members.	A	M	S	R	N
19. Faculty meetings are helpful to me in my current job.	A	M	S	R	N

[End of survey]

Faculty Meeting Rating Survey (continued)

Faculty Meeting Rating Survey Tabulation Form

To obtain a group score from the Faculty Meeting Rating Surveys, follow these directions.

1. Make a copy of the Group Score Tabulation Sheet (p. 141).

2. Tally the group members' survey responses onto the tabulation sheet, using the following scale:

   • Always = 4 points

   • Most of the time = 3 points

   • Sometimes = 2 points

   • Rarely = 1 point

   • Never = 0 points

3. Count the total number of people who responded to each survey statement.

4. Multiply the number of *A* responses by 4, the number of *M* responses by 3, the number of *S* responses by 2, and so on. Insert the results in the relevant cell for each question on the tabulation sheet.

5. Divide the sum total for each question by the total number of respondents.

6. To obtain an average score for each question, round up the number obtained from the previous step to the nearest tenth. Insert this score in the "Average" column.

7. To obtain the overall effectiveness score for the group, add up all of the individual averages and write the total in the space labeled "Group Total."

8. Divide the group total by 19 (total number of questions) and write the result in the space labeled "Group Rating."

9. Use the following scale to help determine areas of strength and areas in need of improvement:

   • Less than 2 = In need of improvement

   • 2.1–2.5 = Marginal, may need to be improved

   • 2.6–3.4 = Average, no need for immediate improvement

   • 3.5–4 = Area of strength

Faculty Meeting Rating Survey (continued)

Group Score Tabulation Sheet

	A (4 points)	M (3 points)	S (2 points)	R (1 point)	N (0 points)	Average
1						
2						
3						
4						
5						
6						
7						
8						
9						
10						
11						
12						
13						
14						
15						
16						
17						
18						
19						
Group Total						
						/19
Group Rating						

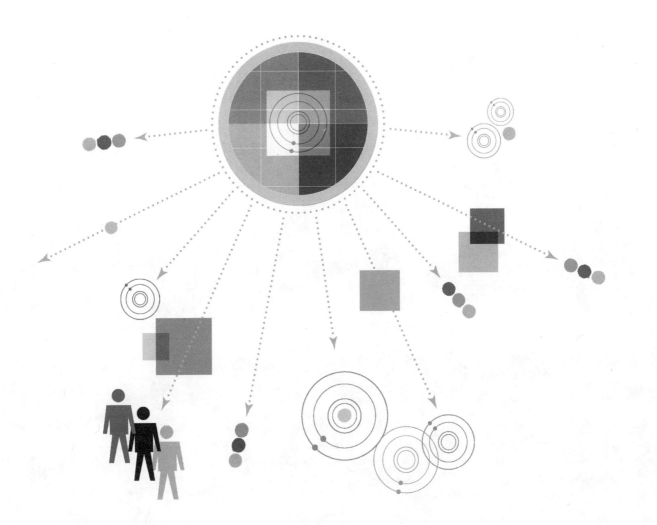

Appendix 2

As a Teammate Form

As a Teammate

Gifts I bring include . . .

Situations I find stressful include . . .

I need to learn more about . . .

I am developing skills in . . .

I can benefit from the following supports:

I can provide the following supports:

Potential Benefits of Inclusion Teaching Teams Form

For Teachers

- Shared decision making, which often leads to better outcomes and results in enhanced motivation
- Increased overall job satisfaction
- Decreased feelings of isolation
- Increased personal and professional development
- Enhanced problem solving through the sharing of diverse perspectives
- _____
- _____
- _____

For Students

- Improved self-concepts
- Fewer removals from the inclusion classroom due to behavioral or learning difficulties
- Improved social skills
- Better relationships between general education students and students with disabilities
- Reduced student-teacher ratio
- Greater academic achievement
- Greater sense of school community
- _____
- _____
- _____

Goals and Parameters Form

Goals

_____

_____

_____

_____

Parameters

Team members must always . . .

_____

_____

_____

Team members must never . . .

_____

_____

_____

Our Vision Form

Keeping in mind the team's goals and parameters, fill out the boxes below.

As an inclusion teaching team, we hope to accomplish the following for *ourselves:*

_____

_____

_____

_____

_____

_____

As an inclusion teaching team, we hope to accomplish the following for *our students:*

_____

_____

_____

_____

_____

_____

Rules and Routines Form

Class: **Teachers:**

Period:

1. Seating Arrangement:

____   Open seating

____   Assigned seating

2. When Entering Class, Students May . . .

____   Visit with friends

____   Place personal belongings on desk and in lockers

____   Place class materials on desk

____   Copy class work assignment from board

____   Copy homework assignment from board

____   Other: _____

3. At the End of the Period, Students May . . .

____   Leave when the bell rings

____   Leave when dismissed by the teacher(s)

4. Procedures for Handing in Completed Work Will Be Discussed . . .

____   Each time work is assigned

____   At the beginning of each class

____   Only when the teacher requests that the work be turned in

5. Procedure for Requesting a Drink of Water: _____

_____

6. Procedure for Visiting the Restroom: _____

_____

7. Procedure for Visiting the Nurse: _____

_____

8. Procedure for Visiting the Principal's Office: _____

_____

Rules and Routines Form (continued)

9. **Procedure for Visiting Lockers:** _____

_____

10. **Procedure for Sharpening Pencils and Requesting Supplies:** _____

_____

11. **Materials Needed for Class:** _____

_____

12. **If Students Are Missing Materials, They May . . .** _____

_____

13. **Procedure for Late Arrivals:** _____

_____

14. **Grading Policy:** _____

_____

15. **Procedure for Making Up Work:** _____

_____

16. **Penalty for Late Work:** _____

_____

17. **Testing Schedule:** _____

_____

18. **Procedure for Asking Questions:** _____

_____

19. **May Students Chew Gum or Have Snacks in Class?** _____

_____

20. **Talking Is Allowed . . .** _____

_____

Roles and Responsibilities Form

Ongoing Roles	General Ed. Teacher	Special Ed. Teacher	Both	Paraprofessional
Monitoring goals for each student with disabilities				
Developing new IEP objectives for students with disabilities				
Planning activities to achieve the goals				
Selecting and organizing instructional materials				
Teaching specific class content				
Teaching study skills and learning strategies				
Collecting data on student performance				
Establishing and implementing grading procedures				
Establishing and implementing a classroom management plan				
Maintaining home contact				
Participating in conferences				
Modifying curriculum, instruction, and materials as necessary				
Designing tests and assignments to meet individual needs				
Directing paraprofessionals, parent volunteers, or other support personnel				
Communicating with appropriate parties regarding the students with disabilities				
Daily Responsibilities	**General Ed. Teacher**	**Special Ed. Teacher**	**Both**	**Paraprofessional**
Attendance				
Field trip money				
Book orders				
Picture money				
Lunch cards				
Walking/picking up students to/from lunch				
Walking/picking up students to/from phys. ed., art, and music				
Opening activities				
Grading papers				
Interim reports				
Stuffing folders				
Maintaining cumulative folders				

IEP Summary Form

Student: _____

IEP Goals (please state concisely and specify assessment method for subject areas)

Subject area: _____
_____
_____

Subject area: _____
_____
_____

Subject area: _____
_____
_____

Subject area: _____
_____
_____

Subject area: _____
_____
_____

Social and Academic Management Needs (please state concisely)
_____
_____

Accommodations (please state concisely)
_____
_____

Special Needs and Additional Comments (please state concisely)
_____
_____

Unit Plan Form

Unit Title: _____ Teachers: _____

Dates: *From* _____ *Until* _____

Big Ideas (Concepts, Principles, and Issues):

Essential Learning Goals (Knowledge, Skills, and Processes):

Extended/Advanced Objectives:

Objectives Adapted for Students with Disabilities:

Learning Strategies to Emphasize:

Concepts to Review:

Activities:

Major Unit Project(s):

Major Unit Project(s) Adapted for Students with Disabilities:

Supplementary Activities:

Assessments:

Assessments Adapted for Students with Disabilities:

Materials Required:

Materials Adapted for Students with Disabilities:

Daily Plan Form

Date:

Subject:

Class Period:

Unit:

Learning Objective:

Purpose:

Anticipatory Set:

Procedures:

Closure:

Homework Assignment(s):

Learning Strategies That the Special Education Teacher Will Stress:

Methods That the Special Education Teacher Will Use to Support and Individualize Instruction:

Methods That Coteachers Will Use to Share Instructional Responsibilities:

Assessment:

Available Resources Form			
Name	**Title**	**How to Access**	**When to Access**

Ongoing Assistance Form

Date	Location	Format	Participation
		Sharing	Required: _____
		Reflection	Optional: _____
		Problem Solving	
		Sharing	Required: _____
		Reflection	Optional: _____
		Problem Solving	
		Sharing	Required: _____
		Reflection	Optional: _____
		Problem Solving	
		Sharing	Required: _____
		Reflection	Optional: _____
		Problem Solving	
		Sharing	Required: _____
		Reflection	Optional: _____
		Problem Solving	
		Sharing	Required: _____
		Reflection	Optional: _____
		Problem Solving	
		Sharing	Required: _____
		Reflection	Optional: _____
		Problem Solving	
		Sharing	Required: _____
		Reflection	Optional: _____
		Problem Solving	
		Sharing	Required: _____
		Reflection	Optional: _____
		Problem Solving	
		Sharing	Required: _____
		Reflection	Optional: _____
		Problem Solving	

Inclusion Teaching Team Reflection Form

Directions: Using this rubric, identify the level at which your team is functioning for each of the indicators listed. When finished, compare your responses with those of your coteacher and identify areas of agreement and disagreement. Decide upon strengths, areas needing improvement, and goals.

(NA) Not Applicable	(B) Beginning	(D) Developing	(A) Advanced

	NA	B	D	A
1. Interpersonal Communication	☐	☐	☐	☐
2. Physical Space	☐	☐	☐	☐
3. Student Arrangement	☐	☐	☐	☐
4. Curriculum Knowledge	☐	☐	☐	☐
5. Curriculum Modification	☐	☐	☐	☐
6. Instructional Planning	☐	☐	☐	☐
7. Instructional Presentation	☐	☐	☐	☐
8. Classroom Management	☐	☐	☐	☐
9. Student-Teacher Interaction	☐	☐	☐	☐
10. Student Assessment	☐	☐	☐	☐

Strengths

_____
_____
_____

Areas Needing Improvement

_____
_____
_____

Goals

_____
_____
_____

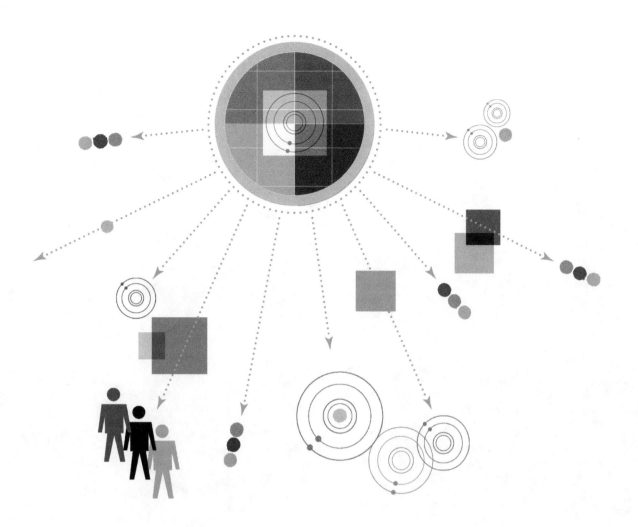

Appendix 3

Worksheet for Establishing and Analyzing Committee or Task Force Work

Directions: Answer the questions below.

1. What is the work to be completed by the team? Be as specific as possible.

_____

_____

_____

_____

2. How will those who receive or review the team's work assess its quality?

_____

_____

_____

_____

3. By when must the team have completed its work? _____

4. Will the level of effort that the team exerts significantly affect the effective completion of its work?

Yes   No

5. Will the amount of knowledge and skill of the team members significantly affect the effective completion of their work?

Yes   No

6. Will the appropriateness of the strategies that the team uses significantly affect the effective completion of its work?

Yes   No

7. Are any of the factors listed in questions 4–6 more critical to the team's work than the other factors? If so, what implications does this have for the design and management of the team?

_____

_____

_____

_____

Worksheet for Allocating Authority for Committees and Task Forces

Directions: Read each statement below and select one response.

1. How much authority will the group need to have in order to complete its work well and on time?

High   Moderate   Low

2. Given the cultural and political realities of the school or district, can the necessary authority be granted to the group?

Yes   No   Not Sure

3. Will group members be willing to operate with the level of authority that *can* be provided?

Yes   No   Not Sure

4. Will group members be *able* to operate with the level of authority that can be provided?

Yes   No   Not Sure

5. Based on the answers to 1–4 above, the group will be:

Administrator-Led   Self-Managing   Self-Designing

6. What implications might the level of authority provided have for the administrator in charge?

_____

_____

_____

_____

Worksheet for Establishing the Advantages, Disadvantages, and Feasibility of Committees and Task Forces

Directions: Answer the questions below.

1. What are the advantages of using a committee or task force to complete the work at hand?

_____

_____

_____

_____

2. What are the disadvantages of using a committee or task force to complete the work at hand?

_____

_____

_____

_____

3. Given that it typically requires more administrative skill and time to manage a group than to manage individuals, do the advantages outlined above outweigh the disadvantages?

Yes   No

4. Given the culture of the school or district and the staff involved, will it be possible to design and support the committee or task force well?

Yes   No

Worksheet for Ensuring Effective Committee or Task Force Composition

Directions: Answer the questions below.

1. How many staff members are required to successfully complete the task at hand?

_____

2. Which staff members have high levels of task-relevant expertise?

_____

_____

_____

_____

3. Of the individuals listed above, which also have at least moderate levels of collaborative skill?

_____

_____

_____

_____

4. Based upon your responses to the questions above, the committee or task force will be composed of the following members:

_____

_____

_____

_____

5. Does this group provide the appropriate balance between homogeneity and heterogeneity?

Yes   No

6. If not, is there anyone from the lists above who could be substituted to improve the diversity of the group's membership?

_____

_____

_____

_____

Worksheet for Designing a Task That Motivates and Engages Committee or Task Force Members

Directions: Answer the questions below.

(For the task to be motivating, the answer to at least one of the first three questions should be "Yes.")

1. Does the task require the use of a variety of skills and talents?

Yes   No

2. Does the task result in a whole, tangible piece of work?

Yes   No

3. Will the outcome of this task make a significant and meaningful difference to the lives of others in the school or district?

Yes   No

4. How can you redesign the task to meet the criteria in questions 1–3?

_____

_____

(The task design must allow for both autonomy and feedback.)

5. Does the task design provide the committee or task force with substantial freedom, independence, and discretion in determining the procedures to be used?

Yes   No

6. Are appropriate feedback mechanisms built into the task so that the group will receive trustworthy feedback?

Yes   No

7. If necessary, how can you redesign the task so that it includes the necessary autonomy and feedback mechanisms?

_____

_____

8. Write a clear, concise description of the task. Include the task requirements, any constraints that may limit group members' options, the material resources available to the group, and who will receive, review, and implement the group's ideas (and what standards they will use to assess them).

_____

_____

Worksheet for Ensuring That the Committee or Task Force Has Access to the Necessary Assistance and Rewards

Directions: Answer the questions below.

1. Can the reward system of the school or district provide the reinforcement the group will need to perform well?

           Yes   No

2. If you answered no above, how can the reward system be modified?

_____

_____

_____

3. Can the information system of the school or district provide the data the group will need to perform well?

           Yes   No

4. If you answered no above, how can the group obtain the necessary data?

_____

_____

_____

5. Can the staff development system of the school or district provide the training the group will need to perform well?

           Yes   No

6. If you answered no above, how can the group obtain access to the necessary training?

_____

_____

_____

7. What resources—space, raw materials, money, tools, or human assistance—will the group need to perform well?

_____

_____

_____

8. Can the resources outlined above be provided to the group?

           Yes   No

Task Definition Form

The task for this committee or task force is . . .

Individual response:

_____

_____

_____

_____

Response with a partner:

_____

_____

_____

_____

Response for a group of four:

_____

_____

_____

_____

Response for two groups of four:

_____

_____

_____

_____

Meeting Log

Date: _____

Members Present	Members Absent	Others Who Should Know About the Meeting

Roles	This Meeting	Next Meeting
Facilitator		
Recorder		
Timekeeper		
Convener		

Agenda Items	Time Limit

Action Items	Person Responsible	By When?

Agenda-Building for Next Meeting

Date: _____   **Time:** _____   **Location:** _____

Expected Agenda Items

1. _____   4. _____

2. _____   5. _____

3. _____   6. _____

Worksheet for Developing a Performance Strategy

Situation (clearly define the task or problem):

_____

_____

_____

Options for Proceeding	Advantages	Disadvantages

Solution (may be a combination of options or a completely new one):

_____

_____

_____

We will know this plan is working when:

_____

_____

_____

Committee or Task Force Rating Survey

Thank you for taking the time to complete this survey about your experience working with this group. Please address *all* of the following statements by circling *one* of the five responses provided in the columns.

A = Always   M = Most of the time   S = Sometimes   R = Rarely   N = Never

1. The group's task was clear.	A	M	S	R	N
2. The group's task was motivating.	A	M	S	R	N
3. The group had the authority necessary to complete the task effectively.	A	M	S	R	N
4. The composition of the group helped members to complete the task effectively.	A	M	S	R	N
5. The group had access to information necessary to complete the task.	A	M	S	R	N
6. The group had access to outside expertise necessary to complete the task.	A	M	S	R	N
7. The group had access to material resources necessary to complete the task.	A	M	S	R	N
8. Group members felt rewarded for completing the task.	A	M	S	R	N
9. Group members clearly understood who was and who wasn't a member of the group.	A	M	S	R	N
10. The group's rules and norms helped members to complete the assigned task.	A	M	S	R	N
11. Members had the opportunity to discuss any barriers to group performance with school leadership.	A	M	S	R	N
12. The group received help that improved its collaborative process.	A	M	S	R	N
13. As a group, members stopped periodically to reflect upon and learn from their experiences.	A	M	S	R	N
14. I found my experience with this group to be personally satisfying.	A	M	S	R	N
15. My experience with this group increased my group work skills.	A	M	S	R	N

[End of survey]

Committee or Task Force Rating Survey (continued)

To obtain a group score from the Committee or Task Force Rating Surveys, follow these directions.

1. Make a copy of the Group Score Tabulation Sheet (p. 172).

2. Tally the group members' survey responses onto the tabulation sheet, using the following scale:
   • Always = 4 points
   • Most of the time = 3 points
   • Sometimes = 2 points
   • Rarely = 1 point
   • Never = 0 points

3. Count the total number of people who responded to each survey statement.

4. Multiply the number of *A* responses by 4, the number of *M* responses by 3, the number of *S* responses by 2, and so on. Insert the results in the relevant cell for each question on the tabulation sheet.

5. Divide the sum total for each question by the total number of respondents.

6. To obtain an average score for each question, round up the number obtained from the previous step to the nearest tenth. Insert this score in the "Average" column.

7. To obtain the overall effectiveness score for the group, add up all of the individual averages and write the total in the space labeled "Group Total."

8. Divide the group total by 15 (total number of questions) and write the result in the space labeled "Group Rating."

9. Use the following scale to help determine areas of strength and areas in need of improvement:
   • Less than 2 = In need of improvement
   • 2.1–2.5 = Marginal, may need to be improved
   • 2.6–3.4 = Average, no need for immediate improvement
   • 3.5–4 = Area of strength

Committee or Task Force Rating Survey (continued)

Group Score Tabulation Sheet

	A (4 points)	M (3 points)	S (2 points)	R (1 point)	N (0 points)	Average
1						
2						
3						
4						
5						
6						
7						
8						
9						
10						
11						
12						
13						
14						
15						
Group Total						
						/15
Group Rating						

Group Presentation Form

Objectives	Action Steps	Individual(s) Responsible	Timeline	Evaluation

Bibliography

Aldage, R. J., & Riggs-Fuller, S. (1993). Beyond fiasco: A reappraisal of the groupthink phenomenon and a new model of group decision processes. *Psychological Bulletin, 113,* 533–552.

Alderfer, C. P. (1977). Group and intergroup relations. In J. R. Hackman & J. L. Suttle (Eds.), *Improving life at work.* Santa Monica, CA: Goodyear.

Anthony, W. P. (1979). Management for more effective staff meetings. *Personnel Journal, 58,* 547–550.

Appelbaum, E., & Batt, R. (1993). Policy levers for high performance production systems. *International Contributions to Labour Studies, 3*(1), 1–30.

Argyris, C. (1983). Action science and intervention. *Journal of Applied Behavioral Science, 19,* 115–135.

Arhar, J. M., Johnston, J. H., & Markle, G. C. (1988). The effects of teaming and other collaborative arrangements. *Middle School Journal, 19*(4), 22–25.

Ashton, P. A., & Webb, R. B. (1986). *Making a difference: Teachers' sense of efficacy and student achievement.* New York: Longman.

Baines, L., Baines, C., & Masterson, C. (1994). Mainstreaming: One school's reality. *Phi Delta Kappan, 76,* 39–40.

Bandura, A. (1982). Self-efficacy mechanism in human agency. *American Psychologist, 37,* 122–147.

Blasé, J., & Blasé, J. (1999). Effective instructional leadership through the teachers' eyes. *The High School Magazine, 7*(1), 17–20.

Brown, S. J., Bartunek, J. M., & Keys, C. B. (1985). Teachers' powerlessness: Peer assessments and own perceptions. *Planning and Change,* 23–33.

Cole, D. A., & Meyer, L. H. (1991). Social integration and severe disabilities: A longitudinal analysis of child outcomes. *The Journal of Special Education, 25,* 340–351.

Cook, L., & Friend, M. (1998). *Interactions: Collaboration skills for school professionals.* White Plains, NY: Longman Publishing Group.

Cragan, J. F., & Wright, D. W. (1991). *Communication in small group discussions: An integrated approach* (3rd ed.). St. Paul, MN: West.

Crow, G. (1998). Implications for leadership in collaborative schools. In D. G. Pounder (Ed.), *Restructuring schools for collaboration: Promises and pitfalls* (pp. 135–154). Albany: State University of New York Press.

Deno, S., Maruyama, G., Espin, C., & Cohen, C. (1990). Educating students with mild disabilities in general education classrooms: Minnesota alternatives. *Exceptional Children, 57,* 150–161.

DeRoche, E. F. (1972). Elementary school faculty meetings: Research and recommendations. *Elementary School Administration,* 40–44.

Drucker, P. F. (1999). *Management challenges for the 21st century.* New York: Harper Business.

DuFour, R. (1986). *Effective business practices can be applied to schools.* Orlando, FL: Secondary School Principals Meeting (ERIC Document Reproduction Service No. ED 269 837).

Eller, J. (2004). *Effective group facilitation in education.* Thousand Oaks, CA: Corwin Press.

England, J. (1996). Teaching team concept helps Missouri district's inclusion effort. *Inclusive Education Programs, 4,* 6–7.

Erb, T. O., & Doda, N. M. (1989). *Team organization: Promise, practices, and possibilities.* Washington, DC:

National Education Association.

Evans, I. M., Salisbury, C., Palombaro, M., & Goldberg, J. S. (1994). Children's perception of fairness in classroom and interpersonal situations involving peers with severe disabilities. *Journal of the Association for Persons with Severe Handicaps, 19,* 326–332.

Evans-Stout, K. (1998). Implications of collaborative instructional practice. In D. G. Pounder (Ed.), *Restructuring schools for collaboration: Promises and pitfalls* (pp. 121–134). Albany: State University of New York Press.

Feyerherm, A. E. (1994). Leadership in collaboration: A longitudinal study of two interorganizational rule-making groups. *Leadership Quarterly, 3*(4), 253–270.

Fiol, C. M. (1994). Consensus, diversity and learning in organizations. *Organization Science, 3,* 403–420.

Fishbaugh, M. S., & Gum, P. (1994). Inclusive education in Billings, Montana: A prototype for rural schools. (ERIC Document Reproduction Service No. ED 369 636)

Friend, M., & Cook, L. (2007). *Interactions: Collaboration skills for school professionals.* Boston: Pearson Education.

Fryxell, D., & Kennedy, C. H. (1995). Placement along the continuum of services and its impact on students' social relationships. *Journal of the Association for Persons with Severe Handicaps, 20,* 259–269.

Garmston, R., & Wellman, B. (1999). *The adaptive school: Developing and facilitating collaborative groups.* Norwood, MA: Christopher-Gordon.

Gass, R. H., & Seiter, J. S. (1999). *Persuasion, social influence, and compliance gaining.* Boston: Allyn & Bacon.

Giangreco, M. F., Dennis, R., Cloninger, C., Edelman, S., & Schattman, R. (1993). "I've counted Jon": Transformational experiences of teachers educating students with disabilities. *Exceptional Children, 59,* 359–370.

Giannangelo, D., & O'Connor, P. (1980). Yawn, sigh, tsk: Teachers rate faculty meetings. *The Executive Educator, 23,* 37.

Gladding, S. T. (1991). *Group work: A counseling specialty.* New York: Macmillan.

Goetz, L. (1994). Evaluating the effects of placement of students with severe disabilities in general education versus special classes. *Journal of the Association for Persons with Severe Handicaps, 19,* 290–301.

Gooden, J., Petrie, G., Lindauer, P., & Richardson, M. (1997). Principals' needs for small-group process skills. *NASSP Bulletin, 82,* 102–107.

Gorton, R., & Burns, J. (1985). Faculty meetings: What do teachers really think of them? *The Clearing House, 59,* 30–32.

Gronn, P. C. (1983). Talk as the work: The accomplishment of school administration. *Administrative Science Quarterly, 28,* 1–21.

Hackman, J. R. (1976). The interaction of task design and group performance strategies in determining group effectiveness: A review and proposed integration. In L. Berkowitz (Ed.), *Advances in experimental social psychology.* New York: Academic Press.

Hackman, J. R. (1987). The design of work teams. In J. W. Lorsch (Ed.), *Handbook of organizational behavior.* Englewood Cliffs, NJ: Prentice-Hall.

Hackman, J. R. (1990). *Groups that work (and those that don't): Creating conditions for effective teamwork.* San Francisco: Jossey-Bass.

Hackman, J. R. (2002). *Leading teams.* Boston: Harvard Business School Press.

Hackman, J. R., & Oldham, G. R. (1980). *Work redesign.* Reading, MA: Addison-Wesley.

Hallinger, P., & Murphy, J. (1986). The social context of effective schools. *American Journal of Education, 94*(3), 328–355.

Harris, T. E., & Sherblom, J. C. (2002). *Small group and team communication.* Boston: Allyn & Bacon.

Helmstetter, E., Peck, C. A., & Giangreco, M. F. (1994). Outcomes of interactions with peers with moderate or severe disabilities: A statewide survey of high school students. *Journal of the Association for Persons with Severe Handicaps, 19,* 263–276.

Hollowood, T. M., Salisbury, C. L., Rainforth, B., & Palombaro, M. (1995). Use of instructional time in classrooms servicing students with and without severe disabilities. *Exceptional Children, 61,* 242–253.

Horlock, C. (1987). Breathing new life into faculty meetings. *Thrust for Educational Leadership, 16,* 36–37.

Hoy, W. K., & Miskel, C. G. (1996). *Educational administration: Theory, research and practice.* New York: McGraw-Hill.

Hunt, P., & Farron-Davis, F. (1992). A preliminary investigation of IEP quality and content associated with placement in general education versus special education classes. *Journal of the Association for Persons with Severe Handicaps, 17,* 247–253.

Hunt, P., Farron-Davis, F., Beckstead, S., Curtis, D., & Goetz, L. (1994). Evaluating the effects of placement of students with severe disabilities in general education versus special classes. *Journal of the Association for Persons with Severe Handicaps, 19,* 200–214.

Hunt, P., Soto, G., Maier, J., & Doering, K. (2003). Collaborative teaming to support students at risk and students with severe disabilities in general education classrooms. *Exceptional Children, 69,* 316–334.

Hunt, P., Staub, D., Alwell, M., & Goetz, L. (1994). Achievement of all students within the context of cooperative learning groups. *Journal of the Association for Persons with Severe Handicaps, 19,* 290–301.

Janis, I. L. (1982). *Groupthink.* Boston: Houghton-Mifflin.

Janney, R. E., & Snell, M. E. (1996). How teachers use peer interactions to include students with moderate and severe disabilities in elementary general education classes. *Journal of the Association for Persons with Severe Handicaps, 21,* 72–80.

Jenkins, J., Jewell, M., Leicester, N., O'Connor, R. E., Jenkins, L., & Troutner, N. M. (1992). Accommodations for individual differences without classroom ability groups: An experiment in school restructuring. *Exceptional Children, 60,* 344–359.

Johnson, D. W., & Johnson, R. T. (1989). Research shows the benefits of adult cooperation. *Educational Leadership, 45,* 27–30.

Johnson, D. W., & Johnson, R. T. (1994a). *Leading the cooperative school.* Edina, MN: Interaction Book Company.

Johnson, D. W., & Johnson, R. T. (1994b). *The nuts and bolts of cooperative learning.* Edina, MN: Interaction Book Company.

Jones, R. (Sept. 1995). Meetings without tedium. *The Executive Educator,* 18–20.

Kaiser, J. (1985). *The principalship.* Minneapolis: Burgess.

Katz, D., & Kahn, R. L. (1978). *The social psychology of organizations.* New York: Wiley.

Katzenbach, J. R. & Smith, D. K. (1993). *The wisdom of teams: Creating the high-performance organization.* Boston: Harvard Business School Press.

Kennedy, C. H., Shukla, S., & Fryxell, D. (1997). Comparing the effects of educational placement on the social relationships of intermediate school students with severe disabilities. *Exceptional Children, 64,* 31–47.

Kohm, B. (2002). Improving faculty conversations. *Educational Leadership, 59,* 31–36.

Leavitt, H. J. (1975). Suppose we took groups seriously. In E. L. Cass & F. G. Zimmer (Eds.), *Man and work in society.* New York: Van Nostrand Reinhold.

Leithwood, K. A., & Riehl, C. (2003). *What we know about successful school leadership.* Philadelphia: Laboratory for Student Success, Temple University.

Levine, D. (1991). Creating effective schools: Findings and implications from research and practice. *Phi Delta Kappan, 75*(5), 389–393.

Lipsky, D., & Gartner, A. (1995). The evaluation of inclusive education programs. *National Center on Educational Restructuring and Inclusion Bulletin, 2*(2), 1–7.

Matthews, J. (1998). Implications for collaborative educator preparation and development: A sample instructional approach. In D. G. Pounder (Ed.), *Restructuring schools for collaboration: Promises and pitfalls* (pp. 155–172). Albany: State University of New York Press.

McFadzean, E., & Nelson, T. (1998). Facilitating problem-solving groups: A conceptual model. *Leadership and Organizational Development Journal, 19,* 6–13.

McGrevin, C., & Lohr, C. (1987). Faculty meetings: An administrative tool for the instructional leader. *The Clearing House, 63,* 70–72.

Murphy, J. (1989). Principal instructional leadership. In P. Thurston & L. Lotto (Eds.), *Advances in educational leadership* (pp. 163–200). Greenwich, CT: JAI Press.

Murray-Seegert, C. (1989). *Nasty girls, thugs and humans like us: Social relations between severely disabled and nondisabled students in high school.* Baltimore: Brookes Publishing.

Nigro, K. (1984). *Developing confidence and self-motivation in teachers: The role of the administrator.* Eastern New Mexico University. (ERIC Document Reproduction Service No. ED 269 842)

Odom, S. L., DeKlyen, M., & Jenkins, J. R. (1984). Integrating handicapped and nonhandicapped preschoolers: Developmental impact on the nonhandicapped children. *Exceptional Children, 51,* 41–49.

Organ, D. W., & Bateman, T. (1996). *Organizational behavior.* Plano, TX: Business Publications.

Pincus, J., & Rayfield, R. (1986). *The relationship between top management communication and organizational effectiveness.* Norman, OK: Public Relations Division Association Convention. (ERIC Reproduction Service No. ED 269 793)

Pounder, D. G. (1998). *Restructuring schools for collaboration: Promises and pitfalls.* Albany: State University of New York Press.

Praisner, C. L. (2003). Attitudes of elementary school principals toward the inclusion of students with disabilities. *Exceptional Children, 69*(2), 135–145.

Qin, Z., Johnson, D., & Johnson, R. (1995). Cooperative versus competitive efforts and problem solving. *Review of Educational Research, 65,* 129–143.

Rea, P. J., McLaughlin, V. L., & Walther-Thomas, C. (2002). Outcomes for students with learning disabilities in inclusive and pullout programs. *Exceptional Children, 68,* 203–224.

Richardson, J. (Oct.–Nov. 1999). Harness the potential of staff meetings. *Tools for Schools, 1*–3.

Riehl, C. (1998). We gather together: Work, discourse, and constitutive social action in elementary school faculty meetings. *Educational Administration Quarterly, 34,* 91–125.

Royal, M. A., & Rossi, R. J. (1996). Individual-level correlates of sense of community: Findings from workplace and school. *Journal of Community Psychology, 24,* 395–416.

Saint-Laurent, L., & Lessard, J. C. (1991). Comparison of three educational programs for students with moderate mental retardation integrated in regular schools. *Education and Training of the Mentally Retarded, 26,* 370–380.

Schwartzman, H. B. (1989). *The meeting: Gatherings in organizations and communities.* New York: Plenum.

Scruggs, T. E., & Mastropieri, M. A. (1996). Teacher perceptions of mainstreaming/inclusion 1958–1995: A research synthesis. *Exceptional Children, 63,* 59–74.

Seamon, D. F. (1981). *Working effectively with task oriented groups.* New York: McGraw-Hill.

Senge, P. M. (1997). Communities of leaders and learners. *Harvard Business Review, 75,* 25–26.

Sharpe, M. N., York, J. L., & Knight, J. (1994). Effects of inclusion on the academic performance of classmates without disabilities. *Remedial and Special Education, 15,* 281–287.

Shelton, M. (1994). *Secrets of highly effective meetings.* Thousand Oaks, CA: Corwin Press.

Sousa, D. A. (2003). *The leadership brain.* Thousand Oaks, CA: Corwin Press.

Staub, D., & Peck, C. A. (1995). What are the outcomes for nondisabled students? *Educational Leadership,* 36–40.

Staub, D., Schwartz, E., Gallucci, C., & Peck, C. (1994). Four portraits of friendship at an inclusive school. *Journal of the Association for Persons with Severe Handicaps, 19,* 314–325.

Tuckman, B. W. (1965). Development sequence in small groups. *Psychological Bulletin, 63,* 384–399.

Villa, R. A., Thousand, J. S., Meyers, H., & Nevin, A. (1996). Teacher and administrator perceptions of heterogeneous education. *Exceptional Children, 63,* 29–45.

Waldron, N. L., & McLeskey, J. (1998). The effects of an inclusive school program on students with mild and severe learning disabilities. *Exceptional Children, 64,* 395–405.

Wanous, J. P. (1994). Effectiveness of problem-solving groups: Process and outcome criteria. *Psychological Reports, 3,* 1139–1153.

Weiss, M. P., & Lloyd, J. W. (2002). Congruence between roles and actions of secondary special educators in co-taught and special education settings. *The Journal of Special Education, 36,* 58–68.

Wheelan, S. (2005). *Faculty groups: From frustration to collaboration.* Thousand Oaks, CA: Corwin Press.

Whitehead, J. L. (1984). *Improving meeting productivity.* American Business Communication Association Southeast Convention. (ERIC Document Reproduction Service No. ED 262 402)

Whyte, G. (1998). Recasting Janis's groupthink model: The key role of collective efficacy in decision fiascoes. *Organizational Behavior and Human Decision Processes, 73*(2–3), 185–209.

Whyte, W. F. (1955). Human relations theory: A progress report. *Harvard Business Review, 34*(5), 125–132.

Wilkinson, A. M., & Smith, M. (1995). Team recruitment, team building and skill development. In H. G. Garner (Ed.), *Teamwork models and experiences in education* (pp. 103–124). Boston: Allyn & Bacon.

Index

Note: Page references followed by *f* refer to figures.

About the Author

Matthew Jennings is currently the assistant superintendent of schools for the Berkeley Heights (New Jersey) Public School System and an adjunct professor at Rutgers University, where he earned his master's degree and a doctorate in educational administration.

In addition to presenting at numerous state and national conferences, the author has served as an organizational behavior consultant to school districts throughout New Jersey. He has worked as an adjunct professor for the College of New Jersey and Centenary College, where he taught courses on school administration and supervision. At the public school level, he has served as a director of student services, a supervisor of curriculum and instruction, and a classroom teacher. His work has been published in *Phi Delta Kappan, Preventing School Failure, The New Jersey English Journal, Channels,* and *The Writing Teacher*. His current research is focused on the leadership of middle school principals in designing and managing interdisciplinary teaching teams.